ulster's
white
negroes

Fionnbarra ÓDochartaigh

Foreword by Bernadette McAliskey,
former Independent MP

AK PRESS

EDINBURGH LONDON SAN FRANCISCO

First printing April 1994

AK Press
22 Lutton Place
Edinburgh
Scotland EH8 9PE

AK Press
PO Box 40682
San Francisco
California 94140-0682, USA

Designed by brian design
Printed and bound in the UK

British Library Cataloguing-in-Publication Data
  A catalogue record for this title is available from the British Library
Library of Congress Cataloging-in-Publication Data
  A catalogue record for this title is available from the Library of Congress

ISBN 1 873176 67 8

Contents

DEDICATION

To the memory of my late father, Harry (d.1989),
a veteran of the Black and Tan War and the Second Defence
of the Republic (1916-1923), who died in his 90th year.

ABBREVIATIONS

ALJ	Association for Legal Justice
BBC	British Broadcasting Corporation
BSR	Birmingham Sound Reproducers
CC	Catholic Curate
CO	Commanding Officer
CR	Civil Rights
CSJ	Campaign for Social Justice in Northern Ireland
DCAC	Derry Citizens' Action Committee
DHAC	Derry Housing Action Committee
DI	District Inspector (RUC)
DUAC	Derry Unemployed Action Committee
f/o	formerly of
GNR	Great Northern Railway
GOC	General Officer Commanding (British forces)
HMP	Her Majesty's Prison
HMSO	Her Majesty's Stationery Office
IRA	Irish Republican Army
IRSP	Irish Republican Socialist Party
IWG	Irish Workers' Group
IWP	Irish Workers' Party (26 Counties)
JCS	James Connolly Society
KKK	Ku Klux Klan
MoD	Ministry of Defence
MP	Member of Parliament
NCCL	National Council for Civil Liberties
NICRA	Northern Ireland Civil Rights Association
NIHE	Northern Ireland Housing Executive
NILP	Northern Ireland Labour Party
NISLL	Northern Ireland Society of Labour Lawyers
NUS	National Union of Students

PD	People's Democracy
PM	Prime Minister
PR	Proportional Representation
RLP	Republican Labour Party
RSF	Republican Sinn Fein
RUC	Royal Ulster Constabulary
SDLP	Social Democratic and Labour Party
SLL	Socialist Labour League (Britain)
UDR	Ulster Defence Regiment
UPV	Ulster Protestant Volunteers
UVF	Ulster Volunteer Force
WTS	Wolfe Tone Society
YRA	Young Republican Association
YS	Young Socialists (NILP)

CHRONOLOGY

1916

Irish Volunteers and Irish Citizen Army join forces and participate in week-long Easter Rebellion in Dublin. Leaders executed, hundreds jailed or interned after this latest abortive attempt to break with the British Empire.

1918

Last all-Ireland general election. Great swing nationally for the ideals of Easter 1916 Proclamation for an Irish Republic. Constitutional nationalists suffer major decline. Sinn Fein attracts major support.

1919

Dail Eireann – an all-Ireland parliament – meets in Dublin. British authorities declare its enactments illegal and launch a campaign of political and military repression. The republican army forged in 1916 responds in defence of the democratic will of the majority and its newly established institutions. The period known as the War of Independence or the Black and Tan War begins.

1921

Britain decides to withdraw from five-sixths of Irish territory. Partition finalised. Republican forces split. Britain arms pro-Treaty forces, and period known as the 'Civil War' or Second Defence of the Republic begins. Stormont rule and the Irish Free State imposed by force of arms on both sides of an artificial border.

1949

Free State ('26 Counties') declared Republic of Ireland. Integration of Stormont statelet ('Six Counties') into the United Kingdom reinforced by British Labour government.

1956-62

Border campaign by Irish Republican Army; internment, as in previous two decades, introduced by both partitionist statelets.

1966

Gusty Spence's loyalist Ulster Volunteer Force guns down four young Catholics in Belfast. An eighteen-year old barman, Peter Ward, is shot dead after leaving work on 26th June.

1967

Northern Ireland Civil Rights Association (NICRA) formed in Belfast.

1968

October 5th: Civil rights march in Derry attacked by RUC.

October 9th: Formation of Derry Citizens' Action Committee (DCAC).

1969

JANUARY: Civil rights 'Students' March' attacked by loyalists at Burntollet Bridge en route from Belfast to Derry. Royal Ulster Constabulary attack Catholic homes in Derry's Bogside during the hours of darkness after marchers reach city.

MARCH: Power station blown up by UVF – IRA blamed by Stormont government, police and British media.

APRIL: Terence O'Neill, 'moderate', succeeded by James Chichester-Clark as Stormont Prime Minister.

JULY: Rioting. Samuel Devenney, 43-year old Catholic, dies in Derry after being savagely beaten in his home three months earlier by the RUC: the first civilian fatality.

AUGUST: Rioting in Belfast and Derry. Battle of the Bogside leads to intervention of British army, first in Derry and then in Belfast. 8,000 soldiers in the six counties of Ulster by the year's end.

OCTOBER: RUC 'B' Specials to be disbanded – and replaced by Ulster Defence Regiment (UDR), under direct British army control. RUC reorganised, supposedly for new role. Constable Victor Arbuckle is shot dead by Belfast loyalists engaged in rioting against disbandment of the 'B' Specials. First RUC fatality.

DECEMBER: Split in IRA – into Provisionals and Officials.

1970

JANUARY: Sinn Fein follows IRA and splits into Provisionals and Officials.

APRIL: UDR inaugurated. British army uses batons and CS gas against nationalist rioters in Belfast, and their General Officer Commanding, GOC

Freeland, threatens to shoot rioters on sight.

JUNE: General election in Britain. Conservatives come to power and nationalists anticipate increased repression. Provisional IRA defend Short Strand enclave from Loyalist attacks.

JULY: British army imposes Whitehall-inspired Falls Road curfew – five Catholics killed, 60 injured and hundreds of homes devastated.

1971

FEBRUARY: Gunner Robert Curtis killed by machine-gun fire in New Lodge Road during major street rioting in this nationalist area: first British soldier to be killed in action by the Provisional IRA – 18 months after troops are deployed.

MARCH: Chichester-Clark replaced by Brian Faulkner as Stormont Prime Minister.

APRIL: Provisionals' bombing offensive begins – 37 explosions in one month.

JULY: British army shoot two youths dead in Derry – three days of rioting. Social Democratic and Labour Party (SDLP) forced to withdraw from Stormont. Bombing campaign intensifies: 91 explosions.

AUGUST: Internment – 340 Catholics and two Protestants detained. Allegations that detainees are being systematically tortured surface. Rioting and street-fighting all over Six Counties. 'No-Go' areas established to defend nationalists from British raiding parties. Loyalists begin a sectarian pogrom in Belfast. In four days, 22 killed – mainly Catholic civilians. Nationalist rent and rates strike begins.

SEPTEMBER: All marches declared illegal – 15,000 attend anti-internment protest in Belfast

DECEMBER: Loyalist pogrom continues in Belfast. McGurk's bar blown up by UVF, 15 Catholics killed. Thirty simultaneous bombings across Six Counties. On Christmas Day, anti-internment march from Belfast to Long Kesh blocked by British occupation forces.

1972

JANUARY: Bloody Sunday in Derry: 13 peaceful civil rights marchers shot dead by the British army. Another died later from his injuries. Some 18 others wounded. The march was against internment and torture. Vast numbers of Irish workers go on general strike until after funerals.

FEBRUARY: British embassy burned down during mass Dublin protests over Bloody Sunday. Campaign of sectarian intimidation in Six Counties

intensifies – many Catholics lose their jobs, several their lives.
MARCH: Stormont minister John Taylor survives Official IRA assassination
attempt. Belfast's Abercorn restaurant bombed – two women killed and
130 injured. Stormont parliament suspended and direct rule imposed by
British Cabinet headed by Conservative Prime Minister, Edward Heath.
William Whitelaw becomes first secretary of state for the Six Counties.

MAPS AND TABLES

MAPS

TABLES

Ireland

DERRY

BELFAST

DUBLIN

The Six Counties

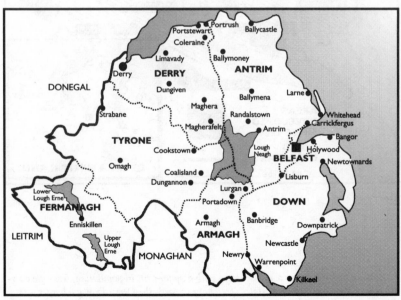

Portstewart Portrush Ballycastle
Coleraine
Limavady Ballymoney
Derry **DERRY** **ANTRIM**
DONEGAL Dungiven
Ballymena Larne
Maghera Randalstown
Strabane Magherafelt Whitehead
Antrim Carrickfergus
TYRONE Bangor
Cookstown Lough Holywood
Neagh **BELFAST**
Omagh Newtownards
Coalisland Lisburn
Dungannon Lurgan
Lower Portadown **DOWN**
Lough Erne
FERMANAGH Armagh Banbridge Downpatrick
Enniskillen **ARMAGH** Newcastle
LEITRIM Upper
Lough Newry Warrenpoint
Erne **MONAGHAN**
Kilkeel

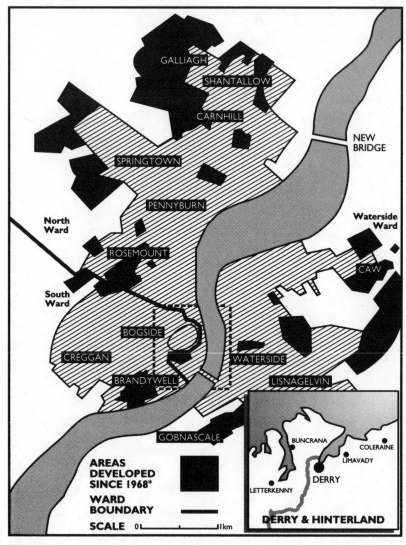

Derry

AREAS DEVELOPED SINCE 1968*

WARD BOUNDARY

SCALE 0 ———— 1km

DERRY & HINTERLAND

* *The boundary extension was associated with a major shift in population, from the overcrowded South Ward to new estates stretching towards the Derry-Donegal border*

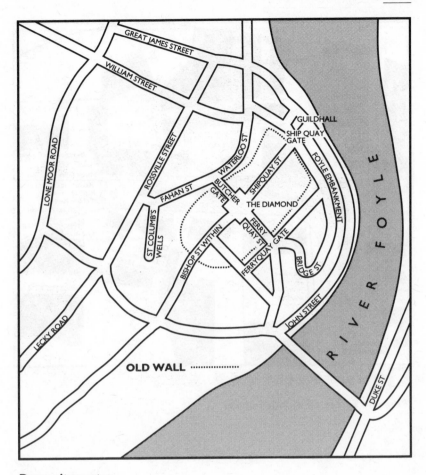

Derry city centre

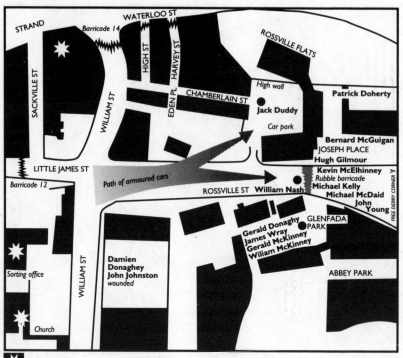

Army sniping positions on high roofs

Rossville Street on Bloody Sunday

Foreword
by Bernadette McAliskey

I had never been in Derry City in my life before October 5th 1968. My only reason for making the journey on that day was to join in the civil rights march. For many years all my visits to that city would be in connection with the struggle for civil and human rights, social and economic equality, self-determination and freedom.

It was in this city that I witnessed some of the most naked brutality of the State and learned, by making mistakes, more than a few hard political lessons.

The vicious attack on the October 5th demonstration by the Royal Ulster Constabulary changed life for all of us. In our political innocence we found the violence of the State almost inexplicable and unsurpassable.

Although we witnessed and were the victims of October 5th 1968, we were astounded and horrified by the police collusion in the 'Burntollet Ambush', where students were savagely attacked, with some eighty-five requiring hospital attention. The occasion was the 'long march' to Derry on January 1st 1969, based on the American civil rights Selma march.

Indeed the title of this book, 'Ulster's White Negroes' – which might strike the reader as a dated terminology – refers to the headline in the London *Sunday Observer* in 1968 after a speech made by Finnbarr O'Doherty comparing the plight of the population of America's black ghettos, the people of South Africa and the nationalist working class in Northern Ireland.

It was in the course of that march that I first met with the author, who spent the marching hours of the three-day trek teaching the rank and file the words and the air of 'The Internationale' which, it seemed to me, only Derry people knew, although there were socialists in Belfast.

The people of the Bogside in Derry were punished for their support of the student march. On the night we arrived in their city, the police attacked the 'ghetto', running rampant through the streets, beating people and damaging property. No-one was ever held accountable for this violence.

As each new level of state violence became commonplace, we continued to be taken aback by new atrocities.

Following my election to Westminster in April 1969, I stood in the high complex of the Rossville Street flats and looked down in despair and disbelief as the police, once again, exacted the penalty from the population of the Bogside who paid dearly for an election victory in which they had not even voted. In the course of that night, the police beat Sam Devenney unconscious as he sat by his own fireside in William Street. He subsequently died as a result. No charges were brought against his attackers.

And so it continued: the three-day siege of the Bogside resulted in the mobilisation of the British army "for weeks rather than months"; and Derry was also the site of one of the earliest 'disputed killings' (or more correctly murders) of civilians, the killing of two young men, Seamus Cusack and Desmond Beattie.

Finnbarr was an integral part of the struggle, from the elections to the barricades, from bulletins and communiques to maintaining communications on his bicycle rounds during the 'Battle of the Bogside', an experience which earned me six months' imprisonment.

Not until the slaughter of thirteen civilians in January 1972 on 'Bloody Sunday' did we finally accept that there was nothing the British government would not do to defeat the nationalist resistance to oppression and our demand for equality.

Born in the Bogside in 1944, Finnbarr is part of the fabric of this city and its politics. The detail with which he records the events before that October demonstration not only places that day in context and illustrates that in Derry, and many other places, a diverse range of political organisations, unemployed, homeless action and social justice groups existed, creating the build-up to 1968, but it restores to their proper place in the scheme of things many activists and organisers who were crucial to this process but remained invisible to an 'image-package' media.

In essence the work focuses on the struggles of ordinary people, mainly within the author's native city, and might be said to be semi-autobiographical.

It is much more than that. The scholarship with which the facts are researched and the sources referred to throughout the text mean that we have here not only a 'primary source' of immense value in itself, but a clear radical perspective, challenging the 'revisionist' trend of historical interpretation, revealing facts and figures otherwise hidden or deliberately ignored.

I have consistently urged all those in struggle, whether in Ireland, Britain or elsewhere, to document and record for the future the history of their own lives and experiences, for this is real history.

It is in sharing the reality of our struggle and experience with those who come after us, or with those who share the same experiences in different contexts today, that we defeat the lies and distortions not only of a simplistic and sensation-seeking media, but of the revisionist, the opportunist and the egotist.

'Ulster's White Negroes' appears at a most crucial period in the development of this, the longest unbroken stage of resistance on this island. While the period covered by the author is essentially that leading up to Bloody Sunday, it is a timely reminder of how the struggle for 'one man–one vote', 'one family–one house', 'one man–one job' became again a demand for an end to British control of Ireland, and self-determination for the Irish people.

It clearly abolishes the pretence that violence in these Six Counties is the cause rather than the result of the problem, and demonstrates the consistent efforts from the community to redress non-violently the injustice of its suffering and protect itself from the violence of the State.

Having read 'Ulster's White Negroes', the reader might well conclude that asking nationalist working class people to recognise 'unionism' as a tradition having equal validity with their own is like asking the Afro-Caribbean, Asian, Indian or Chinese population of the 'United Kingdom' to accord the same dignity to racism.

Finnbarr O'Doherty has, I believe, spent some four years researching and collecting the primary source material for this book, work involving digging out dusty minutes of meetings from plastic bags in the back of cupboards, hours in getting and comparing press clippings, and interviews with ordinary people who remember but whom others forget to ask.

I hope his work inspires others to do likewise.

The events outlined herein, when the history of this whole period is written (devoid of censorship and revisionism) will provide a major part of the explanation of subsequent developments.

In understanding what life was like under the old Stormont regime, the reader will better appreciate the apprehension with which the 'natives' view any political devolution of power to the Northern State and a resurrection of Stormont in any re-vamped version.

Like many of our contemporaries, Finnbarr and I grew up with the struggle, matured with it, and still are young enough in the natural sequence of life to live to see it concluded.

I suspect both of us are born in 'the mould of dissidence' and will continue to organise and agitate in the new dawn.

May both of us, and all those we hold dear, live to see the day. If we don't, may those who come after us read, learn, know and continue to struggle for social justice, equality and human dignity.

Bernadette McAliskey
Co. Tyrone
January 30 1994

ONE

Derry before 'the Troubles'

I n the years leading up to the city's first civil rights march, in
October 1968, Derry City (Londonderry) could best be summed up
in three words, Defeat, Despair and the Dole. The unemployed
made up, on average, 25 per cent of the working population, with male
unemployment as high as 33 per cent. At no time since the inception of
the Six County state had it been lower than 12 per cent and even a
casual observer of social and economic affairs could not fail to see the
blatant disparity between the areas east and west of the River Bann.

Such a situation was not unique to the 1960s, and closer analysis
clearly reveals that behind the rhetoric and triumphalist marches of the
Orange Order and Black Institute, a coldly calculated, sectarian strategy
had been evolving for at least five decades. When the statelet of
'Northern Ireland' was set up in 1921, it contained a population which
was 67 per cent Protestant and Unionist, and 33 per cent Catholic and
nationalist. The Ulster Unionist Party and the British Conservative Party
had successfully defeated the Irish nationalist demands for an independent, united, thirty-two county Ireland, and partition, as the socialist
martyr James Connolly had prophesied, brought its "hey-day of reaction".

The Orange and British Tories have always been conscious of the
need to promote sectarianism in their bid to maintain a weak and
divided working class. Such a device provided a smokescreen behind
which their landed, industrial and speculative elites could keep a firm
grip on the purse-strings, while the masses remained otherwise
distracted and thus allowed themselves to be 'kept in their place'. The
Protestant masses who had supported the Unionist Party, in the main, at

1

the time of the carefully manipulated Home Rule crisis, had to be rewarded for their loyalty to both brands of Toryism. The strategy for such reward was crude, yet simple.

There were no provisions built into the Government of Ireland Act (1920) to safeguard the interests of the native Irish who, north of a line on a map drawn by Britain, had become a fearful and reluctant minority within a partitioned nation and province. Most historians accept that these new boundaries were based on a crude sectarian head-count. By 1923 the Stormont government had in place the framework for a new system of discrimination. Its survival would be guaranteed by Westminster's promise not to raise matters relating to N. Ireland on the floor of the House of Commons. Proportional representation (PR) was erased from the electoral scene. Boundaries were speedily re-drawn as the worst fears of nationalists began to be realised. In Derry City, where anti-unionists had traditionally returned a majority to the local Corporation, ward-rigging reduced the number of nationalist/Sinn Fein representatives dramatically. Put simply, by the mere stroke of a pen, the Unionist minority became the majority on the Corporation, and the nationalist majority became ignored. This was happening elsewhere in 'the North'. It now became possible to implement a strategy of discrimination in the spheres of housing and employment. A battery of repressive legislation, including the Special Powers Act was soon in place, and only Protestants could join a new B-Special police force. All this was to open up a chasm of bitterness, that festered with time.

The denial of electoral equality to Catholics, and the new patterns of discrimination, effectively institutionalised sectarianism to the point of it being considered both 'normal' and 'respectable'. It would in time divide and weaken working class movements overall, as Protestant workers were encouraged to feel superior. The manipulation of housing provision and the labour market would further encourage notions of superiority and comparative prosperity among Protestant workers. Tory power would thus be assured, both in the north of Ireland and in the British parliament. The Blue and Orange Tories' strategy would for future generations provide the added bonus of frustrating the more radical aims and objectives of both the liberal and labour movements in Britain itself.

Discrimination on several fronts against Catholics had the covert aim of encouraging emigration. Catholics were seen as 'a problem' which required a solution. The 'problem' with the Catholic community was that for a mixture of social, religious and economic reasons, Catholics tended to have much larger and more extended families than Protestants, and it was estimated in the early days of the Stormont regime, that within three to four decades they would form 51 per cent of the population. The Catholic surplus had to be effectively drained off, if Tory power was to be maintained. British Conservatives ensured, by a bipartisan agreement with Labour, that the affairs of N. Ireland would not be discussed within the British House of Commons or its 'Upper House'. Such an arrangement held firm until the momentous events of the late 1960s, in which I proudly played a humble part.

According to figures recently published by Queen's sociology lecturer, M. Tomlinson, in the period 1920-1968, 263,000 Catholics left

TABLE 1

(a) Number and percentage of Catholics and Protestants in the six counties, Belfast and Derry City 1911

	Protestant No.	%	Catholic No. (a)	%
Belfast	293,704	75.9	93,243	24.1
Co. Antrim	154,113	79.5	39,751	20.5
Co. Armagh	65,765	54.7	54,526	45.3
Derry City	17,857	43.8	22,923	56.2
Derry County	58,367	58.5	41,478	41.5
Co. Down	139,818	68.4	64,485	31.6
Co. Fermanagh	27,096	43.8	34,740	56.2
Co. Tyrone	63,650	44.6	79,015	55.4

(b) Number and percentage of Catholics and Protestants in the six counties, Belfast and Derry City 1961

	Protestant No.	%	Catholic No. (b)	%
Belfast	301,520	72.5	114,336	27.5
Co. Antrim	206,976	75.6	66,929	24.4
Co. Armagh	61,977	52.7	55,617	47.3
Derry City	17,689	32.9	36,073	67.1
Derry County	64,027	57.4	47,509	42.6
Co. Down	190,676	71.4	76,263	28.6
Co. Fermanagh	24,109	46.8	27,422	53.2
Co. Tyrone	60,521	45.2	73,398	54.8

Sources: (a) Census of Ireland, 1911, Vol. 3, Ulster, Cd. 6051-1, HMSO, London 1912, & (b) General Register Office, Northern Ireland, Census of Population, 1961, County volumes, Tables XVI, HMSO, Belfast 1964.

the North for good, the largest state-sponsored mass deportation of human beings in the Western liberal democratic world during the twentieth century. The policy of discrimination against Catholics was so successful that despite the fact that the Catholic birth-rate was double that of Protestants in the years 1921-68, such does not appear to be the case in the official census figures. Emigration is the only possible explanation. Effectively the Catholic population was kept down to the same level as in 1921.

INDUSTRY

Between 1945 and 1966, out of a total of 224 new industries coming to the Six Counties, only 24 (or nine per cent) were sent to the areas west of the Bann, with only two going to Derry, the second largest city in the statelet. Although the government had the power to influence the location of industries using grants and incentives, not one 'advance factory' – i.e., planned and built before a company was found to occupy it – was built in Derry City until the mid-1960s. Out of the 224 incoming companies, 117 occupied advance factories. There is no doubt that a policy of industrial apartheid had been in operation by the Orange Tory Stormont government since Britain imposed partition in the early 1920s. It was to be used to maintain Unionist power in the predominately pro-partitionist East, because the West, i.e. Derry, Fermanagh and Tyrone, was traditionally pro-nationalist/republican.

TABLE 2

Selected sites for 'advance factories'

Eastern half of 'Ulster'		Western half of 'Ulster'	
Co. Antrim	27	Co. Derry	10
Co. Armagh	10	Derry City	1
Co. Down	17	Co. Tyrone	3
Belfast City	5	Co. Fermanagh	1
Totals:	**59**		**15**

Official report, dated 11.3.69 quoted in The Plain Truth p14, 2nd. Edition, published by the CSJ, 15.6.1969

The extremes to which Unionism would go are exemplified as follows:

The then Minister of Commerce, Brian Faulkner announced on 21st June 1967 the impending arrival of an East German firm to open a factory in Bangor, Co. Down, where, at that time, official figures gave the unemployment figure as 245 persons. On the same date 20 per cent of the people of Derry City were unemployed and in Strabane, Co. Tyrone the rate was 25 per cent. Proof of the existence of such a policy can be obtained by studying the various reports issued by the Six Counties' government over the years. These reports dealt mainly with an area within a 30-mile radius of Belfast, and mentioned only briefly the areas west of the Bann, which seemed to suggest a new partition within the statelet based on geo-political considerations. Not only did the Unionists continue to ignore the need for all types of development in the West, but they dealt the region a series of deliberate body blows during the mid-1960s.

TABLE 3		
Unemployment rates by region (as % of insured population)		
	1951	*1966*
West of the Bann	12.3	10.4
East of the Bann	7.0	5.9
Belfast	4.2	3.7

Source: University of Strathclyde Survey, 1979.

DELIBERATE POLICY

The GNR rail link which transversed the western region was axed, leaving Fermanagh, Tyrone and practically all of County Derry with no rail system whatsoever. The other three counties had two separate systems, one running north from Belfast, and the other south.

In February 1965 the Orange Tories accepted the Lockwood Report, which rejected Derry, the second city, as the site for 'Ulster's' second university. This was in spite of the fact that Magee University College, a century-old institution, was already providing the first two years of university education in certain disciplines, which made Derry the most logical location. In the same month the Stormont government also accepted the Wilson Plan, which outlined four centres for rapid indus-trial development, all of course within the magic radius of Belfast, and none in the western counties which were suffering most from high unemployment.

In order to strengthen further the relatively prosperous east, the Unionists passed plans to build a new city in County Armagh, with the promise that when it was built many industries would fill specially

5

created advance factories. As a further irritant to nationalists it was named after their most famous anti-Catholic leader, Craigavon. In the early period of the plan, an English specialist, Geoffrey Copcutt, was engaged as chief designer and took the post after planning Cumbernauld New Town, near Glasgow. After a year's work he resigned saying, "I have become disenchanted with the Stormont scene." He went on to suggest the abandonment of the new city, and called for the development of Derry City "in order to give the province a reasonable balance". In his statement on education at the time of the Lockwood Report, Mr Copcutt had this to say: "Derry is the obvious choice to expand as the centre of higher education outside Belfast, and would prove the most promising way of unifying the present populations and integrating future immigrant communities." Needless to say, his resignation was speedily accepted by the Stormont regime, which in those days was a power unto itself. Unionism, it seemed, had found both the will and the way to turn its plans for Ulster's new £140m dream city into reality, in spite of the supposed 'lack of resources' which was the usual excuse offered for not promoting the economic regeneration of the region west of the Bann. Their utopian plans were unveiled in a fanfare of publicity in December 1964. This vision of the future was presented in a 126-page report which had taken four years to compile.

This is how the completed city of Craigavon was supposed to look:

• EMPLOYMENT: Realisation of 26,000 jobs between 1965 and 1981, of which 50 per cent were expected to be in manufacturing.

• HOUSING: A total of 18,750 houses were planned. The city housing rate would continue to rise until 1970 when it would be getting into top gear with a rate of 1,500 homes per year.

• EDUCATION: Sixteen primary, eight secondary schools and a new university were to be set in spacious sites.

• LEISURE: Indoor bowling, a theatre, conference hall, museum, art gallery, park, marina, a sports centre with stadium, playing pitches and indoor sports facilities, golf centre and 18-hole course.

• TRANSPORT: A multi-level system of roads to allow cars and lorries to move free from congestion and park or deliver goods easily, along with travelators, escalators, fast, pleasant cycle paths, a rail terminal and a small airstrip

• OTHERS: Seventy-five new churches and a 1,000-bed hospital. The new city would also have its own regional city centre complete with shops and government offices.

GERRYMANDERING

Gerrymandering was one of those 'big words' I overheard while veterans like my father would gather around the fireside to talk of times past or struggles won and lost. A few had gone to defend the Spanish Republic and so other words like 'capitalism', 'imperialism' and 'fascism' entered my vocabulary before I even made my First Communion at the age of seven. When I asked my father what gerrymandering meant, he retorted, "it's a cheap way of denying people their liberties without putting them in jail." My mother had more patience, read from her dictionary and then proceeded to illustrate the point by drawing a map of Derry and placing different numbers inside the boundaries drawn. Put simply, we were like the American Indians who were forced to stay in reservations upon our own stolen lands, dating back some believed to the ÓDochartaighs' revolt in 1608, led by their 21-year-old chief. With the McLaughlins and McDaids we were the last clans to be brutally conquered, with many press-ganged and shipped off to fight in the armies of England's European allies.

I was to learn that electoral ward-rigging was nothing new. As far back as 1840 the Municipal Corporation (Ireland) Act provided a local government vote for all property owners whose dwelling place had a yearly valuation of not less than £10. That restricted franchise was but one device associated with each gerrymander down through the years, as the Catholic population increased in size or influence. When one listened to Unionist spokesmen it all smacked of a form of electoral feudalism, and civic leaders like the mayor would jump up to defend these malpractices. They would talk of the local government electoral system being very broadly based, with the limited company vote, the lodger vote, the ex-service vote and so on. That it tended to favour the propertied classes was made blatantly obvious by comments such as "they who pay the piper were entitled to call the tune." From very early on proportional pepresentation would be a prime objective for key Derry radicals, no matter how 'utopian' or 'ultra-leftist' it seemed then in the mid-1960s.

Things hadn't changed much in thirty years. After a fresh gerrymander in May 1938, the nationalist leader in the Corporation, local solicitor Paddy Maxwell, and MP for Foyle, summed up the situation quite adequately:

> The eight members on my side of the House represent the majority of
> the people; the majority of the Corporation electors because we have

7

2,000 more than all others combined; the majority of the parliamentary electors because we have 5,000 more than all others put together; and the majority of the citizens because we have 29,000, or 11,000 more than all others put together. By a shameless gerrymander scheme, we have been deprived of our rights. The city has been carved up to give an ever-decreasing minority control over an ever-increasing majority. But numbers will tell in the end.

Although the Orange Tories remained a minority in the western counties, in their bid to maintain control over most local councils they continued to manipulate the electoral boundaries long after 1938. These Unionists, by their words and deeds, have never accepted responsibility for the economic affairs of the western region. They obviously viewed their control of such councils as a vital part of their 'industrial apartheid' policy, which was a necessary link to maintaining overall power. Gerrymandering was an essential plank in a general strategy, and for generations had proven to be the most effective weapon of political control in the Orange Tory arsenal. Derry City was the most blatant example of this. In 1966 the adult population was 30,376 – 20,102 Catholics and 10,274 Protestants – yet the Corporation was still Unionist controlled. The restricted franchise was referred to as the 'Company Vote', whereby property owners were allocated several votes, and there was another device that gave the vote only to householders. These complex arrangements had the effect of reducing the Catholic majority substantially so that it became 14,429 Catholics to 8,781 Protestants. With each boundary revision the central aim was the same. In the 1960s the number of electoral wards had been reduced to three:

TABLE 4

South Ward	North Ward	Waterside Ward
11,185 voters	6,476 voters	5,549 voters
10,047 Catholics	2,530 Catholics	1,852 Catholics
1,138 Protestants	3,946 Protestants	3,697 Protestants
8 (Nationalist) Councillors	8 (Unionist) Councillors	4 (Unionist) Councillors

Source: Disturbances in Northern Ireland, Report of the Commission appointed by the Governor of N Ireland (Cameron Report), HMSO, Belfast 1969, Cmd 532, p59, para 134.

'Democracy' in Derry amounted to the nationalist/republican majority returning a mere eight representatives, whereas the supporters of the one-party Unionist regime, which were the minority, returned a staggering twelve. By confining many thousands of nationalists within the South Ward, and by refusing to allocate houses to them in the other two wards (North and Waterside, where the Unionists had majorities), greater miseries were inflicted on the mainly Catholic electorate.

Since the partition of Ireland the Unionists had dived to unbelievable depths to maintain control, particularly in Derry City. There was a separate seat for the city in the early years of the Stormont parliament, and because of the preponderance of Catholics the constituency returned an anti-Unionist member (nationalist). In order to neutralise the seat the electoral division was re-arranged. The city itself was cut in two, Foyle returning a nationalist. The boundary of the city was stretched eight miles into the country, to include pockets of Unionist voters without reference to natural geographical features, in order to scrape together an Orange Tory majority.

HOUSING

During the early Sixties, re-development in the South Ward (where I was born at 134 Bogside) took the form of multi-storey flats, to keep what was effectively a ghetto from expanding. Many who occupied the new flats worried about the increased rent they would have to pay, but they were in heaven compared to those who lived in damp and unhealthy Nissen huts a few miles away at Springtown Camp. These were supposed to be temporary accommodation built for the Allied Forces at the outbreak of World War II, yet were still standing and occupied.

Local government, to put it mildly, left much to be desired. The Derry Corporation Housing Committee did not function for many years. Even attempts by private community groups, such as the Derry Housing Association met with overt and covert political opposition. This association was headed by the late Fr. Anthony Mulvey, truly a pioneer, and it offered a degree of hope for hundreds of homeless families and newly married couples. Its plan was simple, i.e. to build 700 houses. Not surprisingly, permission was steadfastly refused, even though these dwellings were planned on the nationalist west bank of the River Foyle. After some years, a public hearing and countless tedious appeals to the central authority, permission to build a proportion of the number requested was granted. As if to add insult to injury, one person was in total charge of the letting of those few houses actually being built, that being none other than the Unionist mayor of the day.

Although proclaiming their 'Britishness', mayors and Unionist councillors, in the main, refused to implement policies that were commonplace in Britain. There, housing associations, which built houses to supplement local authorities' enterprises, had full co-operation from councils. In the Six Counties they encountered continuous obstruction in an attempt to grind down the will and wreck the spirit of the people. In Co. Tyrone, for example, at least one housing association had to cease functioning after being blocked in three different sites by the Unionist-controlled Dungannon Urban District Council.

When it came to the provision of housing, as in most things, Derry came bottom of the pile as the following comparative analysis reveals.

TABLE 5					
Housing analysis					
Town	Population	Council built	Housing Trust	Total	Per 1000 of 1961 Pop
Coleraine	13,578	833	655	1,488	109
Newry	12,214	1407	358	1,765	144
Portadown	20,710	1196	1069	2,265	109
Larne	17,278	1020	1400	2,420	140
Limavady	4,811	472	186	658	137
Derry City	55,681	2170	1745	3,915	70

Source: DHAC research document

The Londonderry Corporation over the years had refused:

1. to extend the city boundary (there was no room for industry within existing city limits thereby making rates artificially high);

2. to introduce a crash housing programme (over 3,000 on housing waiting list);

3. to build modern roads so as to relieve traffic congestion and improve infrastructure.

Over the years, council experts in city management and the business community, as represented by the Chamber of Commerce, had called for boundary extension. Extending the city boundary raised such issues as rates, housing, industry, and population density, which affected all sections of the local community. Rates in the city were needlessly high because there was no space within the city for industry, which in most towns bears a large share of the burden of rates. All creeds and classes suffered from such negative policies, but the working class suffered worst of all. For the majority there was little hope of a brighter economic future, devoid of narrow sectarian priorities ruthlessly imposed by a small bigoted elite.

There were 3,000 families on the council's housing list, and this list continued to grow rapidly. Thousands were living in miserable conditions because of the lack of land within the city for building homes. Many became the victims of the local Rachmanites* who, together with their gangs of heavies, thrived on the misery of working class families. They charged what they pleased in rent, because the local corporation refused to appoint a rents assessment officer. This was not surprising considering that many of the 'City Fathers' were owners of, or had front-men in charge of, Rachmanite properties, converted into flats mainly for young married couples.

TABLE 6

Analysis of population density

Town	Area (in acres)	1961 Population (pre census)	Density per acre
Derry	2,200	53,762	25
Bangor	2,663	23,862	9
Larne	2,522	16,350	7
Lurgan	2,024	17,870	9
Lisburn	1,957	17,700	9
Coleraine	1,543	11,901	8

Source: DHAC research document, 1968 †

The housing policy of Londonderry Corporation meant that employers were reluctant to come to the city because:

1. there was no space for housing their workers or indeed siting

* Rachmanism, named after an infamous London landlord of the 1950s, refers to the exploitation and intimidation of slum tenants by unscrupulous landlords.

† I must state that I believe these figures relate to a period shortly before the 1961 census, as the population figures for Derry City, Coleraine and Larne are lower than those quoted in the previous housing analysis table. All of the towns, besides Derry City, had extended their boundaries during previous decades. It is worthy of note that nationalist politicians in Derry claimed that the population in the South Ward (Bogside etc) had a density of 125 to the acre. Little wonder therefore that the long-simmering fuse of social revolt would eventually explode from those dimly-lit and narrow proletarian streets of the Bogside.

11

factories;

2. skilled workers were already leaving the city because of the lack of housing and job opportunities for their families.

EMPLOYMENT

In the late 1960s Aidan Corrigan, a civil rights activist from Dungannon, Co.Tyrone, compiled up-to-date facts on Unionist discrimination against Catholics in the North in the spheres of housing, jobs and in the local franchise. His work, 'Eye-Witness in Northern Ireland' focused on Derry County Borough's recruitment policies, which revealed a rather nasty tip to a provincial iceberg that then seemed indestructible.

TABLE 7

Derry County Borough (Population: 68% Catholic)

	Non-Catholic	Catholic
Town Clerk	I	0
City Accountant	I	0
City Surveyor	I	0
Electricity Superintendent	I	0
Director of Education	I	0
Medical Officer	I	0
City Solicitor	I	0
School Dentist	I	0
Sanitary Officer	I	0
Housing Architect	I	0
Welfare Officer	I	0
Housing Manager	I	0
Rate Collector	I	0
Librarian	I	0
Parks Superintendent	I	0

Of the remaining salaried employees of Derry Corporation only 18% were Catholic.

TRADE UNIONS

The position of the trade unions had always been weak in Derry City, because of the high level of unemployment over generations. Workers in the unions made little progress in obtaining an equal wage with their counterparts in Britain, or indeed with their counterparts in Belfast. Many Derry employees were working for wages just above or actually below what they would have received from unemployment benefit. Employers generally took advantage of this situation, and any demand for higher wages or better conditions was met with an attitude of 'like it or lump it', especially in the case of unskilled trade unionists. Derry's capitalists, Orange or Green, were no different in this respect. It was the common practice of some employers to recruit women and youths under the age of 18 so as to obtain the cheapest possible labour-force. It is little wonder that a survey on wealth, carried out in the early 1960s, showed that Derry had more millionaires per acre than any other region in the Six Counties. One leading company, Birmingham Sound Reproducers (later to be called Monarch Electric for tax incentive purposes), continued its 'under 18' policy until late 1966 when they threw 1,500 on the dole with one hour's notice. This clearly showed the weaknesses of trade union representation and their collective lack of clout in the area. However, over several generations, Derry did produce a number of unsung men and women, whose service to the trade union movement and working class aspirations in general was heroic.

Because of these factors, many workers with large families were indifferent to unemployment. They could escape the harsh demands of the employers, and even meagre state benefits provided a higher income than selling one's labour in a low-wage economy. Such men and women could only hope that their children would have a brighter future as they despaired of change ever coming in their own lifetimes.

Single people or those with small families found it difficult to survive on the dole and many opted for the life of enforced exile. Those who stayed at home were naturally resentful, particularly as the 1960s were being hailed as boom years elsewhere in the world. There was, however, still idealism and courage amongst my generation, and even the ever present and threatening dark forces of repression could not deter or eliminate our desire for radical change. From this spring of hope the working class would refresh itself, and prepare to create the much-needed backbone for agitations to come. One of our earliest slogans summed up the spirit of those times: 'Fight Your Corner – Don't Emigrate'.

Here indeed was a vicious circle in which the trade unions were almost powerless. The only rays of hope came with the creation of agitational organisations, such as the 'University for Derry Campaign' in 1964-5, or the Derry Unemployed Action Committee (1965-8) and the Derry Housing Action Committee (1968-71). Several people held dual membership of the latter two committees, including myself. We had long since realised that the two issues were inter-related and could not be divorced from issues relating to electoral malpractices and questions of regional democracy, factors which would eventually decide which forces would hold real power. The slogan of the workless, 'Us Today – You Tomorrow', soon aroused a response, particularly from the youth and even among the skilled unions. Protest marches, pickets, street-corner meetings, occupations and teach-ins were quickly filling our days and nights. These were mainly legal weapons of struggle. Some middle class Catholics approached us to express their fears that 'things might get out of hand someday'. They were quickly reminded that without conflict there could not be change; yet none of us anticipated the brutal reaction that the state would eventually unleash. The grass-roots leaders' desire was that these tactics would evoke an effective response from 'the-powers-that-be'. Our overall long-term strategy was covertly aimed at combating the deliberate policies of neglect adopted by consecutive Stormont governments since the inception of the statelet.

NEW WAVE

By the mid-1960s the ripples on the political pool were clearly visible, to those who wished to see. People were beginning to question the role of their political 'leaders', who were usually from 'Castle Catholic' stock. Our supposed 'betters' had never publicly associated with the unemployed or homeless agitators, except at election times and then only via statements to the press. The day was yet to dawn when such august elements would decide that such a strategy was their only option for survival. However, in the mid-60s liberation theology was unheard of, and the Catholic professional classes viewed social agitation as neither popular nor profitable.

The discontented masses were thus left to their own devices, attracting the occasional blast from the pulpit or several column inches of rebuke in the hope that these might keep us in check. Many of us looked to civil rights struggles in America for our inspiration. We compared ourselves to the poor blacks of the US ghettos and those suffering under the cruel system of apartheid in racist South Africa. Indeed we viewed ourselves as Ulster's white Negroes – a repressed and forgotten dispossessed tribe captured within a bigoted partitionist statelet that no Irish elector had cast a vote to create.

Hundreds of working-class families, who were endeavouring to highlight their conditions around this period, felt they had been both ignored and alienated by respectable, establishment figures. The first wave of articulate youth was beginning to enter the political forum, (some would argue as a direct benefit of the Education Acts of 1944). The 'New Wave' were proudly proletarian and began to question discrimination in employment along sectarian lines. Several became openly involved with working class issues at a grass-roots level. The Catholic middle class were, for the first time, having to compete on an intellectual level with their lesser mortals from the slums. The sons and daughters of labourers could now effectively and passionately articulate the real grievances and feelings of our class. They could even commit these to print by the use of manual duplicating machines, which were frequently moved from safe house to safe house. Such newsletters, which circulated on a door-to-door basis, never lacked ingredients such as a sharp wit, radical songs, satire or poetry. Nationalist leaders and councillors were now being labelled 'Green Tories', whom the young radicals perceived as having a stake in the very system that they chose to attempt to reform from within. The record of these Green Tories had not been dazzling, mainly due to the strength of Unionist determination to maintain the status quo, warts and all. Those who played the 'Orange Card' were fully aware that even minor changes to a strategy that worked for them might prove to be their very undoing. Their mentality has always been summed up as 'Not an inch' and 'No Surrender!', which gave constitutional nationalists few crumbs of comfort to justify their participation within a corrupt political system.

The bogeyman, for both sets of Tories, had always been the republican movement, which locally and nationally attracted a degree of support from the New Wave. The New Wave radicalism was more akin to the teachings of James Connolly than the constitutional nationalism of figures like Daniel O'Connell or John Redmond. We fell somewhere in-between the republican hard-liners and the constitutional one-roaders. Many of us expressed admiration for the disruptive tactics of Parnell in the previous century. The college-educated young radicals together with working-class militants within the local action committees became, in time, a complementary mix. We collectively increased the frequency of ripples upon that long-ignored and politically stagnant pool, which existed in John Bull's own back-yard.

The contemporary republicans were fully conscious of the failings of their militant 1956-62 'Border Campaign'. Those very few who were still active obtained a new zest for action within the agitational movements. They were determined to forge closer links with the people in struggle, in the hope that non-violent action might obtain some remedies which their six year 'war' had failed to achieve. These few veterans were rarely prominent in most of the agitational movements, but their support for reform was later seized upon by the Minister of Home Affairs, William Craig, who played his Orange Card by dubbing the civil rights movement "an IRA front organisation". His aim of course was to weaken the working class solidarity that existed between social activists who embraced different religious creeds or none. Craig particularly wanted to distract non-Catholics from issues such as jobs and homes, which might otherwise act as a community bridge. Class solidarity was always Unionism's second major bogeyman, and the occasional propaganda about Reds and Papist Plots was usually a strong enough cocktail to keep the majority of Protestant workers in a state of bigoted intoxication.

THE FIGHT FOR JOBS
On January 22nd 1965 Quigley's Hotel on Foyle Street became the birthplace of the Derry Unemployed Action Committee. Barely a handful participated in that inaugural meeting, which reflected the deep sense of hopelessness the majority of people felt at that time. We were however determined that we would not be just another flash in the pan; we had to persist, as to do otherwise would further deepen the popular malaise.

Gradually the DUAC expanded with each small successful protest. Public buildings were picketed, council meetings disrupted, teach-ins held within the Labour Exchange at Bishop Street (using its counter as a platform), an unemployed workers' club opened above a dance hall in The Diamond, and the late Brian Faulkner, then Minister of Commerce, received many a stormy 'welcome', as did other notables. On one occasion he was besieged in the Derry Guildhall by 600 chanting demonstrators demanding that he meet a deputation. The mayor refused to convey to the minister the wishes of those of us who had marched from the Labour Exchange. After a lively discussion with colleagues, I took a short stroll, as the DUAC's elected secretary, to the city's General Post Office. No one thought that my cracked proposal would ever work. However, some minutes later, there emerged a whistling, uniformed telegram-boy on a bright soviet-red painted bike who, smiling broadly when cheered by the assembled masses, bore their telegrammed tidings to none other than the Right Honourable Brian Faulkner. The latter, much to our most gracious mayor's obvious annoyance, immediately granted an audience. I recall as we entered the foyer of the Guildhall, where our City Father had previously told us that only over his mayoral dead body would we see the minister, one of the delegation remarked to him, "so it's now a matter of die dog or shit your licence". He had heard his master's voice, was forced to obey, and the timely crack was a further morale booster as we prepared to press the flesh with Unionism's most famous son.

Faulkner had earlier made a statement, on the advice of civil servants, which seriously underestimated the numbers of skilled workers within the ranks of the city's unemployed. This was one bone we were anxious to pick over with him. He agreed to give serious consideration to the findings of a proposed survey which would elicit information on a face-to-face basis with those on the dole. It would seek to establish the real, rather than believed, work experiences and levels of skills within the large pool of unemployed. This was subsequently carried out. Our temporary base was Grant's old disused, snuff factory, immediately next door to the main entrance to the Bishop Street Labour Exchange. Few businessmen would give us the time of day, and may have believed that we were all in receipt of Moscow gold. Grant's permission to use the old snuff factory therefore came as a most welcome surprise. I was later to learn that making money was not the sole priority in life for this businessman, who gave the facilities both gladly and freely.*

This base was essential and we did manage to prove that Derry's unemployed had within their ranks a large percentage of people who had worked at all manner of trades. Their skills were required everywhere but at home. This fact emerged, as had been anticipated by the DUAC leaders. The survey, after further research and analysis, was

---

* John Grant senior had been a nationalist councillor and was the cousin of Tom Doherty, a meat manufacturer and retailer. In the 1930s Tom took up the pen to publish a major thesis on the environment. He had also entered Derry Corporation in 1932 when he began his first three year term of office. My father had entered Tom's company at the age of fourteen at the outbreak of World War I. He eventually threw in his knife and hung up his apron at the age of 79, after some 65 years with this well-known firm. Tom's son James, who followed his father's footsteps into the Corporation in 1950, served until its very last meeting in 1969. It may have been the 'Doherty Connection' that swung the scales in our favour, as this clan has more members in Derry and Donegal than there are lamp-posts, and my involvement may have been made known to Grant through its grapevine. Many Dohertys were in the meat trade. James, in later struggles for reform, would drily remark of the trade and its workers, "The meat is tender, but the men are tough."

personally delivered to the minister as he'd requested, at the parliament buildings at Stormont. After some minutes careful study, he agreed that this had been a worthwhile exercise, which he said would have far-reaching implications, insofar as Derry could be pointed to as having a pool of unemployed with a wide range of skills. These included those used in major industrial spheres such as car production and other areas of engineering and manufacturing. Again, somewhat to our surprise, on future visits to the city Brian Faulkner personally ensured that three executive members of the DUAC would be in attendance at all civic lunches or conferences relating to local economic regeneration matters, where he felt we would have a constructive input. From a nationalist perspective, this was a highly unexpected turn of events from that particular Orange leader, whose rise to fame included being carried on the crest of many a sectarian wave. When it came to economics it looked very much as if he preferred movement on dry land, and our experience suggested that he didn't always accept the word of his civil servants as gospel.

The main officials of the DUAC in those days were Messrs Gerry Mallett (chair), James Gallagher/Bobby Campbell/Ted Bradley (treasurers), Eamonn Melaugh, and myself, holding the positions of public relations officer and honorary secretary respectively.

With a few DUAC activists, including the late Paddy Kirk, I travelled to London to take up a position on the shop floor at Foster's Transformers, Morden Road, in South London. Paddy and myself soon set about the task of establishing an active London branch of the DUAC. We took our message to Speaker's Corner, Hyde Park which attracted some attention from several influential people within the Irish exile community. The Ulster Office was picketed, as part of our efforts to highlight the alleged economic and sectarian apartheid policies by Stormont towards Derry and the other western counties. Selected Labour and Unionist MPs were lobbied at the House of Commons, and obscure socialist groupings extended the occasional invitation to address meetings. I recall how Robin Chichester Clark, our Unionist MP whom we lobbied at the Palace of Westminster, nearly choked over his G&T after ordering us two pints of Guinness in the Members' Bar. The late Paddy Lynch was making a few internationalist comments such as the sad plight of non-white American workers who had recently taken to rioting and burnings in the previously unheard of ghetto called Watts. Paddy was expressing his justified fear that if Unionist leaders did not remove their ear plugs and abandon sectarian notions and economic discrimination, then the natives in our constituency might resort to similar expressions of acute frustration.

The meetings at Hyde Park seemed to reach the people that mattered, and the most notable speakers included Eamonn McCann (best known these days as an author and TV personality), the late Paddy Lynch who attended Queen's University with McCann, Gerry Lawless, Kirk and myself. Over a period of a few weeks some 150 people signed up for membership, but only a hard core remained regularly active. The main base of operation was the Lucas Arms on the Grays Inn Road, near Kings Cross station. The two Irish socialist publications that gave a degree of sympathetic coverage were the *Irish Democrat*, published by the Connolly Association, and the *Irish Militant*, published by the Irish Workers' Group and edited by McCann, ably assisted by Lawless and Lynch.

GOLDEN JUBILEE

In early 1966 there was a Westminster election and the republican standard-bearer was the Tan War veteran Neil Gillespie. It was to be a highly eventful year during which the Young Republican Association (YRA) was founded. What new blood it attracted was soon diluted into the broader, though still small, protest movement. A whole host of publications relating to the post-1962 social and economic policies of the republican movement were being published and more importantly, read. Several others relating to historical figures, such as the trade union leader and socialist revolutionary James Connolly, appeared. Some were published by New Books, based at Pearse Street in Dublin, which had links with the Communist Party of Ireland. The Golden Jubilee celebrations of the 1916 Easter Rebellion in Dublin were a focus of activity.

In London, both Kirk and myself shed a few exile tears as we watched television news-bulletins informing us that a ban had been imposed by the Stormont Minister of Home Affairs on all marches or commemorative events linked to that anniversary. We decided that the sacrifices of 1916 deserved to be remembered, and duly informed our employer that we wanted our cards the next Friday as we were returning home. We stopped in Belfast to see if others shared our anger at the ban before collecting train tickets for 'Dear Old Derry', as Kirk would always describe his birthplace. Soon we were busy organising a parade which attracted a few local bands that were brave enough to

19

participate and some 600 marchers. Transport restrictions under the Special Powers Act had been imposed on cross-border travel as part of a general ban on events associated with the Jubilee. The Unionist leadership wished to give the false impression that such events were only of interest to people living in the South. For the benefit of the outside world and the British public in particular, it was implied that Irish natives north of the border were quite happy and content with all that passed for Unionism's version of British pluralist democracy – without the pluralism.

In the weeks that followed, several republican leaders and activists were charged, including at least one pensioner. Following the republican tradition of not recognising the British courts we boycotted our trials. All were fined. The sum ranged upwards from £5 7s 6d. Some paid their fines (or others paid it for them) which caused some friction and mistrust both within the movement and between the various families. Some believed that the police had paid the fine in one particular case in a bid to discredit a leading member of the movement. I had informed my family that I would not be paying any fine to the British authorities for commemorating men who fought and had their lives forfeited in their bid to remove these same authorities from Irish soil. My father and uncle had been jailed in the 1920s and 1930s as part of that continuing struggle. My older brother had been interned in 1957 and held without charge or trial for three years. He was an art student and was not politically active. It seems he became a suspect because of his intense interest in the language revival movement, the Gaelic League. He refused to sign 'The Paper', the jargon of which assumed you guilty, even though you faced no charge or trial. It mentions cutting all links with listed organisations and the freed internee not participating in illegal political activities. The Paper was a cunning Catch 22. The internees' choices were to sign it and go (which justified the authorities' actions in the first instance) or to refuse and endure imprisonment (with no release date) whilst protesting their innocence. Our family admired my brother's stand.

Doing jail for one's beliefs was nothing new to my family which was highly politically aware and supportive. I had been in charge of the colour-party at the Derry parade and had no illusions as to what would follow such action. Above all I felt non-payment of the fine was the only honourable thing to do, as did my entire family. My immediate relatives advised me on what to expect as I would be a guest of Her Majesty for the first time. My mother packed an old battered suit case, thanking God that at least we could prepare this time as we knew 'they were coming', unlike the internment swoops of the last decade. It was left under the hall table as the arrest date neared.

It appeared that everyone could have their peaceful marches except the natives. Together with the late Michael Montgomery, Kirk and I spent some weeks in HMP Crumlin Road, Belfast during that exceptionally hot and interesting summer of 1966. The night we arrived and the night before being released we were placed in a very large basement cell, with each screw taking the bother to point to a studded, black steel door, telling us that that was the way Tom Williams, a Belfast teenager, passed in the early 1940s to meet the British hangman. The two older men, Kirk and Montgomery had great fun keeping me awake most of the first night. They told one spine-chilling ghost story after another. Before eventually going to sleep they informed me that the screws had slept in their respective beds. When I asked who slept in mine, which was in the middle, the two voices whispered slowly, "the condemned man". Just to add to the special effects one of them bounced an empty tobacco tin off the wall immediately above my bed, which was far from funny in that dimly-lit cell. My whole body seemed to rise in fear a few inches above the mattress. I pretended to be as brave as the young Belfast patriot, Tom Williams, whilst wishing for either sleep or daylight.

During our stay we were to have occasional verbal encounters with the Reverends Paisley, Whylle and Foster* until they learnt that we were not avid members of their growing fan club. They too were guests of Her Majesty for three months. Bewildered English newspapers were carrying reports that these loyalist men-of-the-cloth had grossly insulted their most gracious majesty's Lord Lieutenant and were prominent in the Cromac Square riots. Politically, they were 'on the way up', following a well-trodden sectarian path that had never failed to impress the Orange masses. Gusty Spence was but one member of those masses. Below our barred window he walked, alone with his thoughts. He would use the same exercise yard for many a long year to come. His crime had been the murder of a young, totally apolitical, Catholic barman, Peter Ward, during those infant days of 'Paisleyism' in Belfast.

---

* *Three clerics of Ian Paisley's fundamentalist Free Presbyterian Church. Having established the Church in 1951, Paisley went on to found the ultra-loyalist Democratic Unionist Party in 1971.*

Daily, Paisley and his associates were seen entering and leaving the prison hospital. Prisoners believed that all three worked there, slept there and ate the superior hospital food. It was reputed that Paisley's main task was cutting two and a half pound plain loaves into four. These were called 'eight-ouncers' and were served with a square of butter at meal times. However, there were no tales of loaves, fishes and miracles emanating from the hospital kitchens during our period of incarceration.

The organisers of the 1916 commemoration parade in Belfast included the late Jim Sullivan, Malachy McBurney and Leo Martin, who were also imprisoned with us in Crumlin Road jail. Strangely, these Belfast republicans were incarcerated for a period twice as long as those of us who hailed from Derry. We worked closely together as a team, for at the far end of the wood-yard were a dozen or so Paisleyites with an assortment of sharp cutting implements. In contrast to the leading Cromac Square rioters, we had to labour hard in the open, stripped to the waists, hand-sawing tree trunks or breaking sticks to be bagged. Evidently, even in a northern jail one could not escape from political discrimination.

CIVIL RIGHTS

The YRA in February 1968 assisted in the development of the Derry Housing Action Committee (DHAC) along with radical socialists within the labour and trade union movement. Their attempts to attract the support of the young nationalists for the early protest movements proved abortive, mainly because that body viewed itself as being 'constitutionalists', whose only concern should be 'the Border'.

Direct action remained the strategy adopted by the DHAC. This included opposition to evictions by barricading homes (or helping families back inside their homes after they had been evicted), blocking roads and the occupation of public buildings. The YRA was eventually absorbed into the general protest movement and like many groups seemed to lose the need for a separate structure, identity or label. The seeds sown by a handful of activists over a few short years were to ripen in the form of the emergence of a new umbrella movement, the Northern Ireland Civil Rights Association. Agitational groupings from each of the Six Counties would eventually flock to the NICRA banner. Its creation was a logical consequence of, and reaction to, a growing number of people and groups willing to openly defy the Special Powers

Act, and by so doing challenge the entire Stormont regime. It was not by accident that the slogans of 'One Man – One Job' and 'One Family – One Home' were adopted by the early founders of the civil rights movement, for Derry was seen to have led the way. It was Derry's underprivileged, together with the New Wave, who were to give that embryonic movement both its tongue and eventually its backbone. These latter, essentials for any movement, were rooted in practical experiences of struggle. Outside Derry there seemed to be a genuine fear of pushing the struggle forward at too fast a pace. Several leading individuals expressed reluctance for Derry-style grass-roots politicking, mainly within the Belfast-based NICRA executive. Belfast activists were, of course, in a different situation and knew only too well how sectarian forces could be whipped up in that particular city against even a hint of reform. Derry fortunately had a different experience, and protests there did not provoke any sectarian confrontations.

The fact that the Derry agitational groups assisted people from all sections of the community may have been unique to that city, and no-one could predict what the consequences elsewhere were likely to be. However, once NICRA had agreed to adopt street protests as the best means of highlighting its cause, one could argue that certain elements would use such an eventuality to promote their own brand of religious bigotry. The Stormont regime would also use any excuse to justify future bans and had a history of instigating sectarian conflict when it felt its status quo was under threat.

CONNOLLY

One event in Derry during July 1968 created a high degree of anger and contributed to a new militancy amongst some influential radicals. That event was the Connolly Commemoration, to mark the passing of one hundred years since the birth of the socialist leader and 1916 martyr James Connolly, who was born in the Cowgate area of Edinburgh, Scotland. Ironically, he first came to Ireland as a serving British soldier.

The original plan was to hold a commemorative march, along a non-controversial route on the west bank of the Foyle. I became the main organiser of this commemoration and after some weeks of prep-aration the Minister of Home Affairs stepped in to ban the proposed march. My organising activities were ably assisted by a few former BSR workmates. I broke ranks with the movement over the issue of the proposed flying of the Irish tricolour at this commemoration, which was now threatened by the Stormont ban. We held a minority view that saw the commemoration as a purely proletarian event, rather than a nationalist/republican demonstration. We were opposed to those who seemed incapable of raising their consciousness above that of mere flag-wavers. We felt that only socialist emblems should be displayed, so as to attract all sections of the working class and expose them to the broader radicalism of Connolly's teachings. That the Irish tricolour had been reduced to a sectarian emblem by various Green Tory flag-waving politicians, and had been betrayed by the Irish Free State were factors, for us at least, that diluted its original and honourable revolutionary message. We needed a name, and so the James Connolly Society was formed. The JCS published a special commemorative booklet which was kindly printed on the brand new printing machines at Communist Party HQ in Belfast. This was entitled 'Derry Salutes Connolly'. It contained his portrait and a profile of the leader, as well as several of his, then little-known, quotations. Before its publication a draft was mailed to Connolly's surviving children, three of whom were previously known to me. Their approval was readily given to its contents, and to the plans to mark the centenary of their father's birth in the Maiden City.

Our commemorative plans included a proposed march from Demesne Avenue to Guildhall Square, where a rally would be held. This, for us, was not a provocative march and the decision not to carry the tricolour, for the reasons outlined, made it even less so. Invited speakers included the son of James Connolly, Roddy Connolly, a prominent member of the Irish Labour Party; Gerry Fitt MP (later made a Lord); Betty Sinclair, the secretary of Belfast Trades Council and Ireland's best known Communist; Michael O'Riordan, a veteran of the struggle to maintain the Spanish Republic and the leader of the old Irish Workers' Party (who did not actually attend, but appointed Sam Nolan to speak for the IWP); English-born Janet Wilcock, of the local NILP; and the Derry-born socialist and journalist Eamonn McCann. The commemoration was to be chaired by myself, as the honorary secretary of the JCS. No representative of the Republican Clubs had been appointed to address the gathering because of the continuing flag controversy. Behind the speakers, a large blue double-bed sheet had been turned into a banner bearing seven large white stars in the shape of the plough, which was known commonly as Connolly's Flag or the Plough and the Stars. That was the only flag in sight, as we had determined. It was held firmly by JCS supporters on a high wall, above the speakers and beyond the possible reach of the RUC Special Branch.

After the minister's ban local police chiefs had me brought in to Victoria Barracks where I was informed that a meeting would be permitted, but only at the old Butter Market on Foyle Street. They further stipulated that it should be positioned at least fifty yards from Derry Guildhall. I kept all the intended speakers informed of every major development, and requested that Fitt publicly support the JCS as we did not wish to comply with this latest ban on the right to march. His reaction was crucial for the invited speakers and ourselves. He told me by phone that 'our hour has not yet come', the timing wasn't right, that too few might turn up and that we didn't have the right 'balance of forces' on our side as yet. We were bitterly disappointed that such a leading politician did not approve of our wish to defy the ban but decided that a rally at least would be better than nothing and therefore abandoned plans to hold a march, on Fitt's advice.

On Sunday July 21st, the scheduled day of the meeting, the owner of a coal lorry which was to be used as a platform, was detained by police as he was leaving his home for Foyle Street. The speakers were forced to borrow a rather loose-legged chair from Foyle Taxis nearby. They sometimes had to be physically supported to remain on this makeshift platform, as they addressed several hundred people on that exceptionally hot afternoon.

Our anger at the police was intense, but the Republican Labour Party leader did little to brighten up our day. Connolly's life and ideals took second place as Fitt lambasted the local Nationalist Party and Corporation, then declared that he intended to establish a local branch of his RLP, before ending amid cheers, stating that if he had been organising this commemorative event, the ban would have been defied. This bombshell was unprincipled to say the least. Any respect we had for Fitt vanished instantly, and any hope of setting up a RLP branch was blown out of the window by its own leader. His words made him appear militant, and the JCS appeared cowards by contrast. When I tackled Fitt about his apparent change of heart about defying the ban, he was not in the least apologetic or embarrassed. He merely shrugged his shoulders, shook his head a few seconds, and fixed his eternally loose glasses before abruptly declaring, "Well that's politics, comrade." At that point JCS members swore privately that come the next banned march, Fitt would have the honour of being placed in its front ranks, if he actually turned up and it was ever allowed to move off.

Long after that commemorative event, its organisers and participants were still smarting at state interference and none of us would ever again trust politicians. Fitt and the police had wounded us, yet privately we became determined that the days of accepting bans had now passed, come hell, high water, or the dubious opinions of politicians.

NICRA had, however reluctantly, accepted the need for street protests, and Derry was well represented at their first ever official demonstration from Coalisland to the Market Square, Dungannon, Co. Tyrone. The march was to highlight recent cases of discrimination in relation to housing, and had initially been called by the Dungannon based Campaign for Social Justice. At last things seemed to be improving, as Tyrone activists were at least being allowed to march over a considerable distance, but like us, they were banned from their main square. Besides a few scuffles, the first civil rights march was an outstanding success.

After the August 24th Tyrone demo the call was made by the DHAC to NICRA's Belfast-based executive to hold a civil rights march in Derry. Regardless of the decision of that executive, a handful of leading activists had already begun to plan the city's first march for sometime in October, with the assembly point being the Waterside railway station. We argued that that location would be more convenient for people who had to travel to the march from elsewhere.

However, during all these preparations, we remained anxious to obtain the blessing of NICRA, which in time arrived amid fears, being freely expressed, that there was a major difference between the country lanes of Tyrone and the Maiden City. Saturday 5th October was the agreed date, commencing at 3.30pm, from the Waterside railway station on the east bank. The march was to go to The Diamond, across the River Foyle, where a public meeting was planned. As expected by key organisers, it was duly banned by the Minister of Home Affairs, William Craig. This had been predicted by a radical minority in Derry but seemed to have come as a real shock to the Belfast-based NICRA executive. What happened between the railway station gates and the end of Duke Street can be truly said to be the stuff of history. The civil rights cause that afternoon attracted the missing ingredient that was to turn our agitation into a mass movement literally overnight. This ingredient was the power of modern modes of communication, which brought the thud of the batons, the force of the water-cannon, the cries of the people, and the blood on the tarmac into the very living rooms of millions. The predictions of the few had become reality for the many, as the mask of a one-party police state slipped one afternoon to reveal its true undemocratic and ugly sectarian face.

Sometime next morning, the two Eamonns, McCann and Melaugh, and myself answered the expected knock on our respective front doors. We were taken in police cars to the now demolished Victoria Barracks on Derry's Strand Road. We were placed in one large cell, taken for questioning separately and eventually charged before a special court with being the prime organisers of an illegal civil rights march. Historians now point to October 5th 1968 as the beginning of 'The Troubles'.

TWO

The Harvey Street eviction

I967 was to be a significant year for historians. January witnessed the establishment of a broad front reformist movement. At long last the various strands of protest would be united under one leadership in an attempt to attract a global focus and bring pressure to bear upon the British government. At least that was the intention. We believed that mere exposure of sectarian malpractices in these six north-eastern counties of Ireland would prove to be a major embarrassment for 'the mother of all parliaments', both at home and abroad. The Northern Ireland Civil Rights Association was to be born in the city of Belfast when some forty activists, including myself, met to act as its midwives. The birth was not accompanied by any scream. It went almost unnoticed by the British media, and even some prominent Irish radicals did not think it significant enough to be there to see it take its first gasps of breath or to hear its mild infant cries for reform. Its life was to be dedicated to human progress through the means of non-violent dissent.

Only three people travelled from Derry to attend its founding meeting. They included the English-born Labourite Janet Wilcock, a Dublin-born university economics lecturer, T.A. O'Brien and myself (invited in my capacity as honorary secretary of the Derry Unemployed Action Committee). Our means of transport was an old van which was long past its sell-by date. It stuttered, stopped and started in a most temperamental fashion, totally indifferent it seemed to the fact that Irish history was in the making. Like more than a few local politicians, it belted out a lot of hot air and steam, was not fit enough for the job nor made any sense at all to the non-technical lay-person. The engine had to

29

be cooled down before it eventually felt comfortable and fit enough to splutter on and complete the eighty-odd miles to that once revolutionary city of Belfast.

NICRA was conceived within a united front strategy, whereby a forum was created in which republicans, communists, and community activists could exchange ideas and plan joint activities. It was a miracle in itself that such a strategy would produce anything constructive, as such diverse political tendencies were often anything but comradely towards each other. The writer and playwright, Brendan Behan (1923-64) once wrote that too many formative groups in Ireland could only agree to split at an early stage of hammering out an organisational framework for future activity. Ireland he felt was full of splitters. His words were very much on my mind as we reached Belfast: I was constantly waiting for the character Brendan described to jump up any second and speak those dreaded words, "I propose a split!"

The Wolfe Tone Society (WTS), itself a forum for exchanges of ideas and experiences between radical groupings, had ensured that after months of private meetings agreement could be reached before NICRA was exposed to the glare of publicity and scrutiny. The January launch was minutely planned, and any ideological or personal wrinkles were well and truly ironed out long beforehand. The WTS was considered too high-brow for many rank and file activists. It was most certainly an elite of activists and thinkers, who believed that moral and intellectual force alone would eventually win the day against undemocratic practices and economic injustices. Indeed, in retrospect, we were all idealists then!

Dialogue with the Campaign for Social Justice, led by Dr Conn McCloskey of Dungannon and his wife Patricia, was a crucial part of this overall process. The CSJ had close links with various Westminister MPs and published a regular newsletter, most of which were mailed to prominent figures at home and abroad. All this political intercourse eventually resulted in the birth of NICRA. The infant grouping initially modelled itself on the National Council for Civil Liberties in Britain. It childishly thought that great improvements could be achieved by restricting its programme to handling individual complaints, and that the NCCL approach was sufficient within the local context. Yet it would be a year and more before it was gradually steered towards direct action by way of street politics. Normal democratic pluralism could never work in an abnormal society such as ours. The prospect of taking to the streets was a last resort for the more moderate elements within NICRA, but their pressure group, gradualist approach had been seen to fail. Whatever its strengths and weaknesses, however, NICRA did not emerge from thin air. What follows paints more of the background to the days and years leading up to the creation of the civil rights movement, and offers some explanations as to its subsequent development.

In the early 1960s Republican Clubs were established as a means of getting around the Stormont ban on Sinn Fein and as a means of promoting legal political activities. I became their executive treasurer. When the Republican Clubs in turn were banned, in March 1965, we defied the ban by holding a well publicised meeting. I recall the venue as being St Mary's Hall, built on a laneway in West Belfast where we braced ourselves for the Special Branch to storm the meeting. Sections of the local and foreign media were in attendance. This fact may have influenced police tactics, as their ultimate plan was to be selective, and pick their targets after the meeting ended and the press were gone.

Tom Mitchell (once elected to Westminster for Mid-Ulster, but didn't take his seat), a man called Jordan and myself were apprehended within minutes. We had tried to dodge them by entering the '47 Club in Divis Street. An Irish dancing class was in full swing and bewildered parents froze, not knowing what was afoot. The late Kevin Agnew, who was with us, managed somehow to walk right past them and was not apprehended. Our state visitors may have known that he was a solicitor, and that taking him might be counter-productive as we'd have had a legal adviser at hand. We were taken to a fortress-like police station, which I later learned was Hastings Street, and questioned for several hours. We were released very late at night, not knowing where we had been held. Outside stood a lone figure – and a face that smiled for a change. It belonged to a bespectacled middle aged lady, whose humanity was evident by a parcel under her arm which when opened revealed a large flask of tea and delicious home-made sandwiches. She may never know how welcome a sight she posed, bravely alone that dark night on a Belfast pavement. That image lingers still though almost three decades have passed. I learned later that her name was Mary McGuigan and that she had waited there for many hours before our eventual release.

When it became obvious that the ban would not be lifted on the Republican Clubs, we again tried to get around it by establishing the Young Republican Association in Derry in 1966. Such restrictions on free speech and the right of assembly were but the latest attempt by

Home Affairs Minister Craig to suppress even quite legitimate non-violent opposition to the status quo. The YRA however, to our relief, was never formally banned. Our main propaganda weapon was *Spearhead*, a duplicated newsletter, which sold approximately 2,000 copies on a door to door basis every three weeks. I was its editor.

Since the early 1960s republicans had been engaged in social agitation which included strikes, the right of access to beaches, opposition to ground rents and foreign ownership of land, and such issues as fishing rights. A number of cheap publications were produced to highlight such issues as the movement swung even further to the left during the years that followed its abortive 1956-62 'Border Campaign'. The WTS played a central role in this process, in particular Dr 'Red Roy' Johnson, with whom I worked closely. In later years we parted company when he insisted that all public speakers should demand the democratisation of Stormont rather than its abolition. By that juncture a lot of water had flowed under the bridge and too many of us had come to believe that after almost fifty years of one-party rule the Stormont regime had become irreformable.

Housing was of course always a prime issue in Derry, and was deemed a major priority by the YRA. During the autumn of 1966 a number of evictions had taken place, the majority being carried out by hired 'heavies' engaged by Rachmanite landlords. In September and October many people facing eviction contacted the republican movement and a series of public protests were organised to highlight the plight of hundreds of families who had been on the local corporation housing list, sometimes for as long as fifteen years. The *Derry Journal* of October 7th carried a report of one such demonstration:

> At an open air meeting sponsored by the Derry branch of the Young
> Republican Association on Wednesday night, protests were made against
> the eviction of a young married couple and their two children from a
> corporation owned house at Creggan last week. Paddy Kirk said that the
> eviction laws still operated in Ireland. In Derry Rachmanism was rife, with
> landlords who charged £4.10 shillings a week for one furnished room.
> More evictions were pending and it was time something was done about
> it. Mr Jim Doherty said that their representatives in the Guildhall "would
> be better attending to the interests of the people on issues like this than
> attending functions behind closed doors at which toasts to one of the
> richest women in Europe, the English Queen, were drunk". A petition
> protesting against evictions being carried out where the evicted family

had no alternative accommodation was passed among the attendance
for signature.

For months the YRA spearheaded a campaign in the city against evictions, and, on a few occasions when families were threatened with physical abuse by the 'heavies', republicans stepped in to warn off those making such threats. We sometimes lived with families until the danger of such had passed. Often the very mention of republican assistance was enough to protect the families under threat from the hired thugs. Rather than resort to physical violence ourselves, it was felt that the best way to hit the landlords was through their pockets. The aim also was to improve the lot of their tenants. The worst landlords soon discovered a swarm of officials descending on their properties, reports flying back and forth, many awkward questions to be answered, forms to be completed, and continual time-consuming interviews and meetings to attend. We had taken the trouble to read up on fire regulations, public health requirements and long-forgotten local bye-laws. The end result was a few costly fire escapes being installed, the issue of weekly rent books, the odd bathroom or extra toilet, the closure of several very damp rooms after being deemed 'unfit for human habitation', and several more minor victories for the underdogs. Rachmanism was no longer looking as profitable as before, as the tenants' struggle was becoming both collectivised and sophisticated.

Usually the local Rachmanites bullied their tenants onto the street without even a court order, which would make such acts 'legal'. Because of the high costs involved in legal wrangles, and associated publicity, many working class families were reluctant to seek the aid of solicitors and the courts. The late Kevin Agnew travelled from Maghera, and fought for several families in the full knowledge that they had no means to pay him for his legal services. Often there were as many as nine families in one large terraced house, and all too frequently they shared but one bathroom and toilet. Many were evicted solely to increase profits for the owner who had come across a more desperate family that was willing and able to pay a higher rent. The local council, dominated by conservative elements who had a stake in the status quo, turned a blind eye to these goings on. It was strongly suspected that they or their business associates had money tied up in such properties, and took care to hide behind middle men. On the misery of the homeless, many grew rich. Our moral and political task was now to bring a little discomfort and tension into their petit bourgeois lifestyles.

The Rachmanites became highly irate at our 'interference with private enterprise'. Some even had the audacity to approach some right wing veterans of our movement, who agreed with their complaints, and put it down to the 'young fry' or 'a few Reds that didn't go to Mass'. Very quickly these right wingers were parroting the same phrases as the landlord class, showing just how out of touch they were with post-1962 republicanism. The YRA replied by quoting James Connolly, "Ireland without its people means nothing to me" or "The cause of labour is the cause of Ireland, the cause of Ireland is the cause of labour." Some of the old guard sought to keep the movement both green, respectable and conservative, suitably tailored so as not to upset the influential Catholic middle class, and its cassocked or editorial spokespersons. They declared, somewhat vainly, that "issues such as housing and unemployment have nothing to with republicanism."

The leadership of every branch of the movement, except Sinn Fein, had long since been in the hands of the 'young Turks' who took little notice of their elders, and declined to spend their time in trying to teach old dogs new tricks. The younger generation had totally embraced the finer points of the new social and economic objectives of the post-1962 era and were deeply anxious to see real change in their own lifetimes. Many of the traditionalists, especially in Belfast, were bitterly opposed to that programme, seeing it as 'a new departure'. For us, we felt that every middle-aged woman facing eviction could one day be our own mother and every young couple in a similar plight could easily be our brothers or sisters. Put simply, it was the whole rotten system that was to blame, for it put profit above people, and thus produced such innocent victims in the first place.

RESISTANCE

By the spring of 1967 a tangible wave of discontent spread through the city, and in particular the Bogside district, which was to lead to the formation of the Derry Housing Action Committee. This latest agitational grouping would in time play an important role in the history of the early civil rights struggles. The creation of the DHAC was an illustration of the fact that many working class families began to become more militant in the knowledge that others shared their plight, and that the radical Young Republican leadership would assist them in resisting unjust evictions.

This discontent was to receive an emotional focus when a YRA member stopped to talk to a forty-eight year-old widow. She had been standing at her front door, at number 17 Harvey Street, quietly shedding a few tears out of sight of her two younger children. That chance meeting was to put the name of Ellen (Nelly) McDonnell on the lips of thousands and into the history books. Unlike countless other heads of households who had been faced with the threat of eviction, she did not intend to leave her home meekly like a lamb. Her determined fight to maintain her home is now not merely a matter of local history. Her stand was to educate the wider public in those previously unseen and unspoken horrors associated with the eviction process. Nelly McDonnell faced the ordeal, although she had been in poor health for many years. Her heroic stand forced evictions and other working class issues onto the agenda of those struggling for civil rights and equality. Others benefited directly from her brave stance, as for more than a decade, her name and that of Harvey Street were popularly recalled as 'Derry's Last Eviction'.

Nelly McDonnell's husband had been a British soldier, who had died prematurely. During World War II, while serving with the Allied Forces in the North African deserts, he sustained major shrapnel wounds. Her particular situation was discussed by all branches of the republican movement locally, and positive action to highlight her dilemma was approved with little hesitation. The fact that the family had lived at the same address for many years, and that Nelly had personally cared for her husband and other relations until their deaths, were major factors in lending her active support. A twenty-four hour picket was placed on the house, and placard-carrying youths paraded the street to further highlight the family's dire plight. Many neighbours came forward to convey verbal support, and others provided tea and sandwiches, or fish and chips, to the picketers, who duplicated and distributed hundreds of leaflets. Towards Christmas, due to mounting public pressure, a stay of execution was obtained from the courts. A lull in the struggle came which was to last several months. The *Belfast Telegraph* of July 11th 1967 reported:

> Crowds gathered in Harvey Street, Derry, this afternoon as Young
> Republicans moved barricades into the house of widow Ellen McDonnell
> who with her family faces an eviction threat. Inside, six young republicans
> played records through an open upstairs window and prepared "for three
> months' siege if necessary". Mrs McDonnell said, "I would leave without
> any trouble if I thought I was wrong. I have been on the Housing Trust
> list for 19 years," she added. "About 40 of us will maintain a vigil in

shifts", said a YRA spokesman. "Last night we began barricading. We don't know when the bailiffs will come. I suppose it will be after they are finished with the other eviction in the Bogside."

Lending his skills to the barricading effort was Gerry Mallett, an out of work joiner. He was the recognised leader of the city's Unemployed Action Committee, which had previously expressed its support to the family. Another frequent visitor who managed a passage through the internal barricades was Gerry 'the Bird' Doherty. Born in Eglinton, Co. Derry in 1911, he had become a living legend for republicans throughout Ireland. Gerry spent many hours giving moral and practical support to Nelly throughout her long ordeal. His presence was appreciated by the younger activists as it showed that at least a few of the 'old guard' were on the side of the underdogs. Gerry, who sadly departed life's struggle in May 1993, was an inspiration to all who had the honour to know him. Good humour and tenacity always characterised his recollection of successive phases of the struggle in which he took part. He had seen the inside of more than one jail, and being dissatisfied with the conditions and general service at Crumlin Road in June 1941, he decided to seek out alternative accommodation. Before abruptly abandoning His Majesty's hospitality, his good humour again shone brightly, being thoughtful enough to leave a message scrawled on his cell wall for the screws. It read simply, "The Bird has flown."

On July 12th, as tens of thousands of Orangemen paraded on nearby Derry Walls, the task of barricading had been successfully completed. A large banner was placed along the front of the dwelling which carried the message 'No Surrender!' This of course attracted the attention of many curious Orangemen who ventured beyond Castle Gate to see why such a slogan should appear in a nationalist street. Their puzzlement was extreme enough for them to personally enquire. When the case was explained by Nelly's young defenders, several Orangemen donated quite generously to the campaign without gaining any knowledge of the exact politics of those who gratefully accepted their cash. This incident would be recalled with much amusement for many a long year afterwards.

Meanwhile, moves were afoot to force the local council to give the family a new home, or at least provide immediate alternative accommodation, and legal advisors were engaged for that purpose. On August 1st 1967, on legal advice, the YRA withdrew from number 17 Harvey Street as a hearing was to take place in a Belfast court the following day. Their legal advisors indicated that there were high hopes of success as the local council was duty bound 'to provide alternative accommodation under statute law'. The case was to be held in the morning, but not before an RUC Special Branch man, posing as an inspector from the electricity department, was admitted to the house, supposedly to read the meter. Once he established that no republicans were in the dwelling, the street was invaded by police cars and bailiffs who began to break down the front door, while the family were still in bed. On hearing the rattle of axes and crowbars, Nelly, daughter Susan and son Billy, began to reinforce the barricades and effectively blocked off the stairs while the agents of the state, some forty in all, gradually gained entry.

The *Irish News* of August 3rd 1967, under the heading, 'Captain Boycott Tactics in Eviction of Derry Widow', stated:

> The Republican Labour Party in Belfast lashed out last night at the Captain Boycott tactics of yesterday's eviction in Derry of 48 year-old widow, Mrs Ellen McDonnell and her 13 year-old son. Mrs McDonnell threw cups, plates and cutlery at police after a violent struggle on the top floor. "It is tragic," said Councillor Paddy Kennedy, "that in this day and age, regardless of the heartlessness surrounding this eviction, a young boy should be maltreated by the police for doing what was in fact the most natural thing in the world... defending and helping his widowed mother in her hour of need. The fact that the poor woman also suffered a heart complaint and had to be taken to hospital from the house in an ambulance, is a tragic reflection on the disregard of the law for the personal and human element involved. Surely," added Cllr. Kennedy, "the days of Captain Boycott should be over."

That same report captured some of the drama of the day. When news reached me that the eviction was taking place I headed straight for Harvey Street. As usual I was very conservatively dressed in a three-piece suit, white shirt and tie, carrying a smart old-style leather briefcase that Mrs McDonnell gave me months before to attend meetings. I somehow managed to so impress the police (much to the amusement of the crowd), that without any words being passed they immediately broke their chain of linked elbows. They clearly assumed I was a civil servant of one department or another. I kept a strict poker-face with great difficulty. Now inside that semi-circle of constables and DIs, separating the large crowd from the bailiffs and dwelling, I suddenly leaped onto the front window sill. The semi-circle remained positively frozen and gob-smacked as the 'civil servant' began to address two audiences. One was composed of amused locals and the other, bewildered uniformed servants of the Crown who began to feel positively inept. The *Irish News* elaborated:

> Bailiffs moved furniture on to the street, and after a short time ejected Billy McDonnell. He returned to the house, however, but after a fierce struggle police brought him outside again and frog-marched him down the street. A 200 strong crowd cheered when Mrs McDonnell began throwing crockery and cutlery. They booed the bailiffs. As the eviction was being carried out, members of the Young Republican Association arrived, and one of them spoke to the crowd from a downstairs window sill. He said, "Fellow citizens, today we have witnessed an eviction which could not have taken place across the water. This is owing to the laws which are in force in this area, laws which have been kept on the Statute Book by the Housing Executive and Stormont authorities." After verbally attacking the police for their ill-treatment of Billy McDonnell, he called on the people to lodge a protest at Victoria (RUC) Barracks and was later held there, together with another man who had entered to lodge the complaint.

Within weeks of the Harvey Street eviction, homeless families began to organise more effectively. Immediately on arrival at hospital Mrs McDonnell was told by sympathetic doctors that they would only release her when the local authorities provided her and her children with suitable accommodation. Within a matter of days the family was reunited. With the prior assistance of veteran republicans such as Paddy Kirk and Michael Montgomery, who had set about repairing damaged furniture and making the flat ship-shape, her new house began to look like a home. Mrs McDonnell had no work to face as she turned the key of her new abode and the tea-cups were soon filled and the chat flowed. She loved Aran Court, even though it was directly above a shopping complex. Her front window overlooked a large green field at the far edge of which stood the main church in the Creggan district, St Mary's. Now viewed as a woman of much courage, who had taken a stand for the wider community, as well as herself, she was warmly welcomed by local residents. There she remained amongst them in the Creggan estate until her sudden demise in the mid-1970s. Nelly had become a working class hero out of sheer necessity.

THREE

The homeless revolt

On a cold February day in 1968, four women and two men sat in the Corporation Housing Department reception. They were discussing the overall housing situation in the city, and in particular the plight of the four women present, all of whom then lived in flats at Limavady Road. Within the previous few days their landlord had cut off their electricity and they were forced to live in candle-lit rooms and cook on open fires. Their family doctors were concerned at the potential dangers inherent in such intimidatory practices, and all those involved therefore hoped for positive action from the local city council. This was the beginning of the Derry Housing Action Committee (DHAC), which grew dramatically from that small group of people which included Mrs McNamee and her friends Mrs Dillon, Mrs Olpherty and Mrs Quigley, all with young families. The two young men were Danny 'The Red' McGinley and an English-born Magee University College lecturer, Stewart Crehan PhD, a member of the Socialist Labour League (later to become the Workers' Revolutionary Party in Britain).

Meetings to organise the homeless were held in flats at Limavady Road, and at Stewart Crehan's small flat at 90 Beechwood Avenue. The inaugural meeting of the DHAC was held at the City Hotel on St Patrick's Day weekend. A resolution was passed urging all present to go to March's monthly meeting of Derry Corporation where they hoped to read a prepared address. If not permitted to do so, they intended to disrupt the proceedings to alert the general public to the plight of hundreds of homeless families. This type of activity was frequently adopted by the DHAC, even up to the final meeting of the old

Corporation, which was abolished and replaced by a Commission in March 1969. Few would dispute that the DHAC, and its allies, played a highly significant role in the eventual downfall of that undemocratic and sectarian local assembly.

The first three months of DHAC activity could be described as strictly within the law. I was one of those members who felt strongly that such action was too mild, considering the plight of hundreds of families, across the religious divide, who naturally yearned for the rapid attainment of better living conditions. It was not until a high degree of mobilisation was achieved, through hard daily effort, that such a strategy became possible. This involved extensive leafleting and door-to-door canvassing, with the occasional street-corner meeting. In time, the DHAC leadership began to feel confident enough to embark upon a much more radical programme of action.

The first really militant action took place on June 22nd at 11am, when a caravan home belonging to a family called Wilson was dragged across the main Lone Moor Road to Guildhall bus route at the junction of Hamilton Street and Ann Street in the nationalist Brandywell district of the city. The *Irish Militant* newspaper (Vol. III No. 6), published by the Irish Workers' Group later reported:

> Mr Wilson, an unemployed labourer, who has not had a job since he returned from England four years ago, said the caravan had no lavatory or running water and when the bed was down the living space for four people was about one square yard. His wife, Billie, said she had recently given birth to a baby which died within eight hours, and according to her doctor this was due to the conditions in which the family lived.

There was much local empathy for this particular family and there were no objections from local residents although they suffered some inconvenience as a result of our protests. The mobile dwelling remained an obstruction for some hours on the 22nd, and blocked the road again on the 29th and 30th of the same month.

The local authorities were in no doubt as to the aims and membership of the DHAC. The plan to replace one hard-line Orange Tory with another as mayor, without any changes to the status quo, led to intense vocal protests in the Guildhall council chamber. On the departure of Albert Anderson as mayor it became clear that a new militancy had emerged from the city's slums and ghettos. Frank Curran's book, 'Derry, Countdown to Disaster' (Gill & Macmillan, 1986), notes that: "Nationalist councillor Eugene O'Hare had described the outgoing mayor as 'an implacable, not-an-inch Unionist'."

The mayor symbolised all that the homeless detested about local politics, because he had major powers in the sphere of house building and allocation. These powers were not about to change. Curran's book continues:

> The appointment of Anderson's successor as first citizen led to unruly scenes in the Guildhall. When the Unionists proposed councillor William Beatty, people in the crowded gallery hurled abuse at both Anderson and Beatty. Anderson reacted by proposing the council go into committee, with the press being allowed to remain. Public hostility increased and the Unionists called the police. On arrival, they made it plain they would use force to clear the chamber if necessary. The public agreed to leave, but several men made it clear by word and gesture that they "were not finished with the Unionist councillors". With the public out, and the doors closed, the Unionists elected Beatty who thus made history by becoming the first person to be elected mayor in camera.

Curran, a veteran journalist, and others were in no doubt as to the sharp spearhead that had been forged some weeks earlier. He comments in his book, written years after the event:

> Members of the Derry Housing Action Committee, a new left wing pressure group not to be confused with Father Mulvey's Housing Association, who had been in the public gallery, issued a statement saying that they had withdrawn from the council chamber: "When supporters of the Nationalist Party disrupted the proceedings, we did not want to be involved in another pseudo-sectarian Puck Fair. Furthermore, it is the policy of this Committee to go through all existing channels to have our demands met before taking extreme action. We made our final appeal to the Corporation yesterday. It was totally unsatisfactory."

Not long after the 'caravan affair' the authorities were to react by using the legal powers available to them. Eleven leading DHAC activists were singled out for attention, each to receive a summons demanding an appearance before the Bishop Street Court in July. These were listed in the group's newspaper, *Reality* No. 7, as follows:

> George Finnbarr O'Doherty (23) our Hon. Secretary and Editor; John White (21) a leading member of the Young Republican Association; Eamonn McCann (25) a journalist; Eamonn Melaugh (35) a community worker; Matthew O'Leary, an engineer; John Wilson (28) whose family's 'home' had blocked the road; Jeremiah Mallett (43) a life-long labour

activist and a leader of the unemployed; John McShane (35) a Waterside businessman, as well as Pat J. Coyle (33), and Robert Mitchell (19).

Reality No. 7 reported also that the only woman to appear was an English woman, Janet Wilcock, who had recently carried the Labour Party standard in the Stormont by-election. It reported that:

All were bound over for a period of two years to keep the peace and Melaugh, McCann, White and Wilson were fined £10 each, and Mitchell and Wilcock £5 each.

The *Derry Journal* of Friday, 7th July 1968 ran the headline: 'Corporation flayed in caravan protest case – patience was exhausted says defence solicitor'. Its front-page story continued:

Members of the DHAC and others who blocked Lecky Road with a caravan as a housing protest recently may have taken the law into their own hands, but their patience was exhausted by the failure of Derry Corporation to remedy the "scandalous" conditions in which the occupants of the caravan had to live, a solicitor told Derry Petty Sessions court yesterday.

The DHAC members were ably defended by the republican and civil rights lawyer Kevin Agnew. He ventured the opinion, during a lengthy submission, that they might not have reached the end of the protests because "something had to be done to get a bit of justice from the Guildhall."

The whole incident was yet another small victory for the homeless. The propaganda value increased further when the Wilson family were allocated much more suitable and healthier accommodation at 417 Bishop Street, near their families and friends, yet not far from the mucky lane where their lone caravan home had stood for too long.

If the authorities had hoped to silence the DHAC by using the strong arm of the law, then they knew little of the psychological make-up or political determination of those directly involved. In that respect they failed miserably. Many in the group were both unrepentant and unremitting and one of the most dramatic protests to date took place on the very day the court hearings were in progress. The event was the official opening of the lower deck of Craigavon Bridge, spanning the River Foyle, which divides the city in more ways than one. The mayor and guest dignitaries were confronted by protesters. At a prearranged signal, all sat down on the disused railway tracks, which ran along the centre of the lower deck, effectively blocking a string of quality automobiles. The car owners hoped to be numbered amongst the first-ever to use the new highway, following slavishly after the mayor of course.

This defiant handful included J.J. O'Hara, (whose older brother Patsy was to die on hunger strike in Long Kesh in May 1981); Tony O'Doherty, the distribution manager of *Reality*; Roddy O'Carlin and Neill O'Donnell – both Young Republicans – and lastly Sean McGeehan who was new to the campaigning life. The RUC were taken by surprise, having been outflanked in front of the city's supposed elite. With clearly visible anger they moved briskly to remove the peaceful demonstrators. Now it was the turn of those still standing to play their part. All began to sing a newly-imported song from Black America, 'We Shall Overcome'. As promised, I stepped forward to assume the role of conductor and prompter, as only a few knew the words of the song. During the first verse, RUC personnel rushed towards the small choir and removed me from this cultural activity. The singers bravely continued, with even stronger voices in spite of such philistine interruptions. *Reality* elaborated:

> At this a non-member of the DHAC, one John Lafferty obstructed
> Sergeant Albert Joseph Taylor in the execution of his duty. His umbrella
> had been used for purposes other than it had been designed for. All were
> taken away in police cars and in the less 'comfortable' tenders
> to the 'Vic'.

This primary source informs us also that Neill O'Donnell and Roddy O'Carlin refused to sign a bail bond to 'keep the peace' and so each served a period of one month in HMP Belfast. Their imprisonment was to spark off a chain of protests in many areas, and several radical organisations held pickets in Belfast, London and Cork. On the evening of their eventual release a group of DHAC members and supporters met them at the Waterside railway station, and carried them shoulder high for some distance whilst giving 'victory signs' to the watching police. An informal party awaited them at the Harps Hall, outside which the caravan protest had been held earlier.

Regular picketing of Rachmanites and public buildings continued for several months. *Reality*, the official organ of the group which began as a duplicated hand-out, was now going up-market, carrying interviews and illustrations. It was kindly printed on the Communist Party presses at their Albert Bridge Road offices in Belfast, a detail known only to the chosen few. This publication was the prime source of fund-raising, at a time when some 1,650 families were listed as homeless. Public meetings were held to increase membership and to keep the families informed of what further actions the Committee intended to take as part of their militant strategy. Rent strikes were also organised so as to force the Rachmanite landlords to install fire escapes in the larger tenement houses and issue all families with rent books, which gave some rights in law.

Reality reported:

> Many it seemed would never give in to these demands, but as time passed each broke down rather than end up without their rents paid weekly by the homeless. Repairs were also demanded, and one landlord had to put up £1,000 for one of his tenements.

The latter was after pressure from the health authorities.

It should be noted that the DHAC described all families on housing waiting lists as 'homeless'. It was felt that this was a correct description insofar as each family wished to have a home of their own. Such housing they felt was being denied them because of blatant religious discrimination, political blocking tactics against proposed developments by various housing associations, and the refusal by Unionist-controlled councils to undertake crash house building programmes.

I travelled widely, sometimes as far away as Dublin, to assist local action committees and address rallies. The people of Tyrone were having their own struggle against acute homelessness and blatant discrimination. The Tyrone activists spoke highly of our activities in Derry and looked to us for guidance and solidarity as our experience and numbers were greater than theirs. In Caledon, Co. Tyrone, the local Republican Club was giving support to homeless Catholic families who had begun to squat in newly-built council houses. In June 1968, a Catholic family was evicted from a council house in which they had been squatting. A nineteen-year-old single Protestant, Emily Beattie, secretary to a local Unionist politician, was allocated the house.

As in Derry, the homeless in Tyrone firmly believed that the local Nationalist Party were not prepared to be even good nuisances on their behalf. We collectively held the view that this party was as effective as a chocolate fireguard. I was told that some of the younger members had spirit, yet only one of these, Austin Currie, a Nationalist MP in Stormont, who had been raising the matter, occupied the house in protest and was evicted and fined. His unexpected protest attracted wide publicity and did much to highlight the cause of the homeless, simply because he was an MP. The Campaign for Social Justice in Dungannon soon afterwards called on the NICRA executive to hold its first civil rights demonstration, i.e. to change tack and take to the streets. The reason for the protest was to highlight further the sectarian housing policies in Tyrone and elsewhere.

When the CSJ approached the DHAC for support we immediately replied that we would be at the proposed march with our newly painted banners. NICRA reluctantly fell into line. Paisley's UPV immediately called a counter-demonstration and promised violence if the march from Coalisland entered the Market Square, Dungannon. The RUC duly announced that the march would be re-routed from the centre of the town.

So on August 24th we hired a bus to Coalisland as promised. The actual march was a determined yet good humoured affair. It was met by some flag-waving opposition in Dungannon Square which resulted in some minor scuffles. Paisley had mustered some 1,500 UPV counter-demonstrators, many of them members of the B Specials. In the Square they waited to attack the civil rights demonstrators who numbered between 3,000 and 4,000. At the police barriers the march stopped and a rally was held. After the speeches the civil rights leaders advised the marchers to go home. Instead, the majority of the crowd stayed sitting on the road and began to sing or recite poems. Many stayed there quite late into the night until all the counter-demonstrators had gone, some, like Paisley, having to travel as far east as Ballymena. In the main, it was deemed a major success as it passed off peacefully. This was due in no small measure to effective stewarding by some 70 members of the banned Republican Clubs aided by local people.

Three days after the first civil rights march there were angry scenes as the DHAC and its allies in the Londonderry Labour Party continued the class war from the public gallery of Derry Corporation. The interruptions were fierce and many before police rushed to the Guildhall to usher demonstrators towards the hall and doorways. Away from the view of police, Mayor Beatty was jeered and buffeted and after entering his car attempts were made to overturn it. Some thought he looked as if he was having a heart-attack and urged moderation and that he be allowed to escape popular justice. It was certainly a badly shaken and ashen-faced driver that was allowed to move through lines of outraged citizens who continued to insult him by giving him the Nazi salute. Most felt he had been let off too lightly by far. A short time later his Corporation housing sub-committee announced plans to build 505 houses. This was a futile gesture and merely encouraged an intensification of the struggle.

Things were moving quickly towards a more serious phase. On our return from Dungannon the call was made by the DHAC, to the NICRA executive, to host a similar demonstration locally. This in effect would be Derry's first-ever official civil rights demo. The DHAC's status within the broader Six County protest movement was considerable. This was due in no small measure to the existence of several non-paid, full-time officials, including myself. It was viewed as the reformist vanguard, over and above any of the political groupings in the Maiden City. Some of its leaders were part of a wider network of contacts and groups and dialogue was continuous, revolving around social and economic matters of mutual interest at local, regional and national levels. Within the Left there was of course the usual antagonism between those who considered themselves Trotskyites and others whom they termed Stalinists etc. These factional disputes remained genuinely comradely and were not disruptive to the broader movement as a whole. Such finer points of Marxist dogma or strategy were confined to a minority. The rank and file had more pressing matters of concern, to get their very own key and a roof over their heads.

In a matter of a few short weeks plans were being made for the civil rights march. Eventually NICRA's Executive Committee settled a date after consultation with Derry activists: Saturday October 5th was ultimately agreed for the demonstration. The organising meetings were held in the upstairs lounges of either the Grandstand or Lion bars in William Street, and when larger numbers were expected from afar, the venue was moved to the City Hotel (this hotel was next-door to the Guildhall and near the local bus terminals). At one meeting, for demonstration stewards, only 57 attended and the funds for defraying organising expenses initially came out of the local organisers' own pockets. Most of us were unemployed. A couple were mature students like myself (I had returned in September to full-time education to study for an OND in business studies at the Londonderry Technical College, in a bid to get university entry qualifications). Some organisations which had promised financial support failed to deliver, and in consequence we had to return to our class roots. The bulk of the finances required were collected on a door-to-door basis in the working class Creggan estate. The collection books were later to reveal that those who contributed most generously came from the poorer area of the estate, known as 'The Heights'.

At no stage did activities stop merely because of the planned civil rights demo. Indeed, we were conscious of the need to keep up the pressure as a means of mobilising for October, therefore the next regular meeting of the Corporation was again targeted. Our tactics this time would be different however: we were to remain silent until a given signal. As the Corporation reached the end of its agenda, placard sticks were silently pushed through the ornate handles of the chamber's doors. All present were told they could not leave until we said so and that they would listen to the homeless for a change. One Unionist tried to contact police from a phone on the mayor's bench. He and the phone were quickly seized. He was warned, in no uncertain terms, by one of our larger comrades that if he tried that trick again he would have his arm broken. He returned sharpishly to his seat as per instructions. An 84-year-old Unionist former-mayor, who had previously been knighted for his services to the Crown, was permitted to move into an adjoining room after his younger colleagues pleaded with us that the sight before his eyes might be too much for him to bear. The councillors sat fuming. When the Guildhall clock above us loudly struck two bells, we informed all present that the assembly was now dismissed. One Unionist was heard to whisper softly, "the lunatics have taken over the asylum." I tapped his shoulder to politely inform him, "we lunatics are only looking for a bit of civic sanity from you asylum keepers. And if we don't get it soon you'll all be confronting even less controlled lunatics than us." Highly embarrassed at being overheard he mumbled simply, "I suppose you're right." This incident and others I duly noted in my diary at the end of yet another constructive day.

Elsewhere things were moving along smoothly. Placards were being produced by a sub-committee operating from the home of Norman Walmsley, who rented a house at Long Tower Street. Work there often went on well into the early hours. This was particularly true at weekends, and throughout his son and two daughters ably assisted with the art work. Mickey Devine, then not quite 15, was one young person who aided the effort. He knew all about bad housing, having been born on 26th May 1954 at Springtown Camp. He much later married Norman's youngest daughter whom he met at this time. 'Red Mickey' was to be the last of ten heroic prisoners-of-war who died on hunger-strike in 1981, in their bid to win five basic demands. This 'placards' sub-committee was instructed by two of the key organisers as to what the slogans should be. These slogans reflected what seemed then to be mere utopian dreams. The reality was that Derry was hoping to stretch the civil rights demands and present these as short, sharp slogans, easily understood by the person-in-the-street. 'Proportional Representation' or just 'PR' was one that was indeed short, but would have major long-term implications. All concerned, however, remained ever mindful of the need not to antagonise the NICRA leadership in Belfast who would not see the slogans until the scheduled march assembled.

Little did the bulk of those preparing for the march realise that October 5th 1968 would be entered in the pages of history as a major watershed, or that at long last the local people of Derry would arise from almost fifty years of relative slumber. It should be remembered that the march nearly never happened. A few days before the scheduled date, Home Affairs Minister William Craig banned the march. I personally was delighted at his stupid over-reaction as I knew this would result in increased publicity and a larger turn-out. Leading members of NICRA's executive panicked. They were quickly on the phone, arranging a meeting at the City Hotel which had Fred Heatley, from Belfast, in the chair. The Derry organisers were instructed to inform their respective organisations and supporters to be at the hotel on the evening of October 4th.

At the meeting the executive attempted to convince local activists that the march should be abandoned. Dungannon, they argued, had been legal. Calling off the march would have put the local protest movement further back than it was when it first emerged a handful of years before. Several people like me felt that the bubble would eventually burst, and we were merely assisting fate to decide the time and place to stick the pin. More felt that a U-turn could only benefit the Stormont regime and that only international outrage would ever force a British government, Tory or Labour, to act on our justified demands. The proceedings lasted about two hours and were attended by about 70 people. The debate was heated and frequently punctuated by applause. There was at least one adjournment as members of NICRA's executive went into conclave. The respective Derry groups followed this example and held our own counter-conclaves. The key Derry organisers held firm. The NICRA executive broke ranks after it was made clear in a speech from the floor by Eamonn McCann that we would march without them. All the spokespersons, like good politicians, emerged from the meeting saying that in the final analysis it was "unanimously decided to proceed from the railway station to The Diamond on the route scheduled."

What the NICRA executive had belatedly realised was already knowledge to a handful of the local organisers, i.e. that Stormont wasn't bluffing about meeting our reformist movement head-on. They were determined, in our opinion, to make it impossible for a peaceful righting of wrongs. This was not to be a well-conducted trade union march that merely wished to obtain short-term benefits for workers temporarily upset with capitalism. It was a demo organised for long-term social and economic objectives that would undermine, if not destroy completely, the Stormont status quo. What passed for reform in Britain was being viewed as revolutionary by die-hard 'not-an-inch' Unionist ministers. The regular arrests, which included McCann and myself, gave other key organisers a sense of the fearful anticipation that was building up behind the scenes. The colder than usual demeanour of District Inspector Ross McGimpsey pointed to things getting very hot indeed. In his upstairs office at the rear of the old Victoria Barracks, he acted the civilised state official as, on more than one occasion, he served us up white coffee with sugar and Jaffa cakes. I was pulled in that often he knew how much milk and sugar I liked, when he poured, and how partial I was to the RUC's Jaffa cakes. Although not one to smile much, if at all, he was looking more and more like a man under strong political pressure as the march date approached. Even a blind man would have sensed that the Stormont elite were not at all amused. It was this DI McGimpsey who was clearly seen using his black-thorn stick to impress upon the natives his hostility to their demands. The DI's attitude had been barely concealed during previous visits to his office. His ruthless conduct was dramatically captured by the television cameras for posterity, as he lost his cap as well as his cool. The fact that the organisers would never enter his police barracks voluntarily, when politely requested, was always a source of annoyance to him. This was shown at the end of each cat-and-mouse game which involved his uniformed and plain-clothes men being deployed to 'bring in' selected civil rights organisers.

After our homes or our usual haunts had been visited, they would tour the streets, from which we would be picked up, more often than not, while chin-wagging with somebody, or on the way to yet another meeting with the homeless, unemployed or Labour Party etc. (There was always a daily flurry of activity within and between these respective organisations, and the key figures of each were in constant dialogue). The end result of the police chase would always be the same – when we mice were cornered, we would go quietly. The DI's agenda over coffee was usually associated with possible alternative routes. All too frequent reminders were given of the far reaching provisions of the Special Powers Act. We were usually also told of the alleged fears of local businessmen and their organisations, and how they believed that 'certain marches' would seriously undermine commercial activity if permitted to proceed within the centre of the city. In effect we were being asked to put individual profits before collective rights. There was little doubt that after each meeting at Victoria Barracks the phones would be humming at RUC headquarters in Lisburn, and subsequently Stormont Castle.

Based on the experiences of these involuntary encounters over coffee, it soon became abundantly clear that there should be a maximum mobilisation of media personnel at Duke Street, in the Waterside, on that Saturday afternoon of October 5th. By prior arrangement several were to point their cameras from upper floor windows, while others would be at the front and rear of the demonstration. Thus, this time at least, the outside world would have an unique opportunity of seeing at first hand how the nationalist minority and other disaffected sections of the proletariat were being treated in a supposedly democratic-pluralist society, for which Britain was ultimately responsible.

The Derry Labour Party reflected the views and mood of all local activists in a press statement:

> We welcome the unanimous decision of the meeting to adhere to the original plan. We greet this as a decision by the working class of Derry in all its organisations to assert their rights, come hell, high water or Herr William Craig. No-one has the right to decide where, when and by what route the working people of Derry shall assert their fundamental right to walk through their own city. No-one will set a limit to the march of our class. We are not asking for our rights, we are taking them, and we ask the people of Derry to come with us.

The night before the march an English-born woodwork teacher gave me a crash helmet, at the back of which he painted an eye. He said he wouldn't be marching as it might affect his job prospects, but that he and his wife believed I should wear it as they didn't trust the RUC to act like British bobbies. I had stayed at another address the night before the demo and awoke wondering if the other organisers had been taken from their own beds and held. I feared that I might be alone, and could be seized on the way to the assembly point and that those assembled would be left totally leaderless and confused, and could thus be easily dispersed. I wondered if the full complement of the NICRA executive would even turn up; I felt I knew which ones most certainly would.

I checked a lot of things by phone. The promised three Labour Party MPs had flown in to act as 'observers' in spite of the rising tension. These included Anne Kerr, member for Rochester; her husband Russell Kerr, member for Feltham, Middlesex; and John Ryan, member for Uxbridge. They had been invited over by Gerry Fitt, MP for West Belfast. Surely now, some people remarked on the phone, the police would think twice about attacking the march. They had hoped Bill Craig, who was reputed to be a heavy drinker, wasn't drunk when he gave final instructions to the police. My retort was that whatever happened, one could hardly blame alcohol as bigots were eternally drunk with hate. Many failed to understand the distinction between parliament and the state, and had overrated the importance of MPs. An assortment of the far right Monday Club of Liverpool, the Murray Club and some other sections of the local Orange Order had met and caught taxis at the railway station to be left off at the Apprentice Boys' Memorial Hall, just inside the ancient walls. It was their supposed planned opposition and previous press release that gave the Minister of Home Affairs his much needed excuse to ban the demo. October 5th had never been a traditional Orange marching day, no doubt Craig also knew that this was all a bluff. Kevin Agnew in a letter to the *Derry Journal*, published three days later, remarked:

> Everyone knows that there was no intention on the part of the
> Apprentice Boys to hold a march from Waterside railway station to their
> hall off Bishop Street. I need not waste time and space on this aspect.

Many Protestants were also homeless and had been assisted by the DHAC. Several were to comment privately that it was paradoxical for the Orange Order to claim to defend religious and civil liberties, yet allow their name to be associated with a hard-line minority engaged in the mechanics of their denial. Only liberally-minded Protestants expected anything better from that quarter as their propaganda was never taken very seriously by those in the working class ghettos. We viewed them as similar to the KKK – so bare-faced and confident enough in the bigoted status quo that they wore bowler hats and sashes rather than white robes and pointed hoods. That for generations they had insisted in strutting through Catholic areas, playing sectarian tunes, gesturing and being foul-mouthed (with full police back-up) reveals what the Black and Orange movements are really all about!

As I arrived at the railway station most of my earlier fears soon disappeared as I recognised several friendly faces. Soon I saw my mother and father, both now 'senior citizens' and my youngest brother near the gates. We exchanged concerned glances, as my mother pointed from right to left at several grey-haired people in the assembling crowd, and even some youngsters. Someone I recognised from my BSR factory days shouted, "fasten that helmet, you'll be needing that eye on the back." With my crash helmet firmly strapped, I strolled around observing as the crowd gathered, in time growing to between 350 and 400. Across the river some 10,000 people were gathering for a football match at Brandywell. There was no promised counter-demonstration as I expected. Some 250 police were on duty in the immediate vicinity of the railway station. They had blocked off Distillery Brae with a rope, making it obvious that this first part of the route into Spencer Road was being denied us. To reinforce this point a barricade of police tenders was drawn up behind the rope. It was evident that they wished the march to flow along Duke Street, which in those days offered neither a lane nor an alleyway as a potential exit point.

The tension increased as the RUC made an eleventh-hour appeal. County Inspector William Meharg read the prohibition order to the crowd: "We want to give a warning specially to those who are not interested, for their own safety and the safety of women and children." His message needed no elaboration.

The historian Fred Heatley, the NICRA treasurer, said: "The whole issue is now in the hands of the police. They might let us through, they may try to stop us. If there is any trouble in Derry the blame rests solely with Bill Craig (Home Affairs Minister). We are prepared for a peaceful march."

We organisers quickly regrouped. A last-minute decision was made to switch the route from Distillery Brae and Spencer Road to Duke Street. The police must have assumed that we would take the Distillery Brae route and confront them there. If we had, there were several more points of exit. There was an immediate and hasty change of action on the part of the police as their riot squads jumped into tenders and drove to block off the mouth of Duke Street at its junction with Craigavon Bridge. By the time we reached that police line the parade, led by the 'Civil Rights' banner carried by DHAC members, had grown to around one thousand strong. The 'Fifty Days Revolution', which would end with the Six Counties' biggest ever programme of reform had begun.

In as orderly a fashion as possible we moved slowly while keeping up our spirits and strengthening our resolve by singing 'We Shall Overcome'. We were conscious that immediately behind us the police were on foot and their large water cannon began to move after us as we progressed towards Craigavon Bridge. It was as if we were caught in a long tunnel with both ends effectively blocked, turning it into a human trap. It was not a nice experience, yet there was no choice. It had to be endured as bravely as possible as part payment for a degree of social justice.

We were stopped at the end of the street. As the opposing sides clashed there was a scuffle during which Gerry Fitt MP was targeted. He was the first to suffer a head wound from a police baton. Other politicians under the leading banner were also struck, but not as seriously. Fitt was whisked away by police to their Strand Road barracks and then taken to hospital. The majority of the crowd were unaware of what had happened as the police action had occurred in a few brief seconds. NICRA leaders began to address the crowd. Fred Heatley, NICRA treasurer, and Erskine Holmes from the Belfast NILP were seized by police and placed under custody in a tender. The prime organisers moved towards the middle of the march so as to better observe and decide on what tactics to adopt. Attempts to break through the police lines failed and the marchers began to chant "Sieg Heil!" For half an hour the position remained static. As the marchers held a meeting on the spot, police formed another barricade at the rear of the parade, packing us more tightly into their repressive tunnel.

Several speakers, including the Stormont MP for the city, Eddie McAteer, spoke to the crowd and made appeals to the police for common sense. Other voices raised included those of Austin Currie MP, Ivan Cooper (whom I first met when he was a leading Young Unionist before being converted to socialism and the NILP), and Eamonn Melaugh of the DHAC. I remember also Betty Sinclair, secretary of Belfast Trade Council speaking, and that her strange advice then was to "Go home" just before all hell let loose.

Police and marchers clashed brutally and bloodily within seconds of the last speaker's words being uttered. We had advanced into a wall of police and tenders, with only our fists and feet against batons and strong water jets. Martin Cowley, an 18-year old reporter with the *Derry Journal* was viciously attacked even while he held a notebook in his hand and was shouting "Press, Press!" Other pressmen were to report seeing an obviously pregnant woman kicked, a small boy that just managed to escape and other uncivilised conduct amid the blood and confusion. Shop keepers dragged the injured indoors to give what first-aid they could before later managing to get them through the police lines to hospital. People caught up in the police onslaught screamed as they tried to get away and Eddie McAteer shouted at police as we both witnessed a woman being struck in the mouth by a baton.

The police water cannons were now brought into action and rather than stay still, these were driven through the crowd at speed. Both their jets were spraying at full pressure, enough to throw someone off their feet and push them along bodily for some distance. Behind these came a large number of Stormont's storm troopers, all wearing their brand new steel-helmets with shining black batons swinging. The fact that the force was more than 90 per cent Unionist could account for the partisan viciousness displayed, although two Catholic policemen were said later to have been in charge of at least one water cannon. Now the assault came from both ends of Duke Street as we marchers broke up in a desperate bid to find a way through the police barricades.

The water cannon continually swept both sides of the street. Media personnel who could be identified were particular targets. One water cannon, on returning from the bridge, elevated its line of fire to direct a jet through an open window on the first floor of a house where a television cameraman was filming the proceedings. It then returned again to Craigavon Bridge, with its jets hosing the footpaths. Even the afternoon shoppers, who had not taken part in our demonstration, were not to be spared. Hundreds were sprayed and soaked, including women accompanied by young children or babes in arms. I remember the water being brownish and foul smelling, and it certainly wasn't drinking water. Even as far as the roundabout on the city side of the bridge, more than a quarter of a mile from Duke Street, many were outraged at being caught in the deluge. Stormont had given the green light to their Orange bullies. They had been let loose and everywhere was their playground, and their immediate superiors, including DI McGimpsey, showed no intention of flashing the red stop sign.

Meanwhile, the bitter clash continued in Duke Street. As a result of police action about thirty people were treated in hospital for head wounds before we marchers finally dispersed. Several sought attention in their own homes, shop doorways or made their way to the City

Hotel. The number of injured was later put as high as 88. However, either through accident or design, none of the British Labour MPs were seriously hurt. They were brave enough to go to the main hospital to watch and interview the injured being brought in. They told the press that they were shocked at what they had witnessed and would not care to comment further until they had made a full report to Jim Callaghan, then Labour Home Secretary. Anne Kerr MP was less restrained and explained how she had escaped into a cafe, after being soaked. She spoke of young girls, drenched and injured, entering the same cafe before adding: "The police were grinning and appeared to be enjoying their work."

Next morning, readers of the influential Sunday paper, *The Observer*, were presented with a major report on page 2, written by Mary Holland. She was unique insofar as she seemed to be the only English journalist who had previously bothered to enquire about the realities of life in this region. The civil rights cause had found an influential supporter as her pen was drawn into action on the side of democratic progress. She hastily sent her report after the baton charges at Duke Street. It arrived in time to roll off the presses during the pre-dawn hours. Its headlines read: 'JOHN BULL'S WHITE GHETTOS – Reporting on Ulster's homeless; Houses in N. Ireland are a crucial political weapon, and people don't get houses if they don't vote the right way." She had accurately aimed her literary hammer and thus hit the nail well and truly on the head for her, mainly English, liberally-minded readership.

That same Sunday was not a day of rest for either the RUC or large numbers of youthful citizens. I arose early so as to be washed and dressed and have a hearty breakfast before my expected visitors arrived. They came early as usual and looked in a foul mood, as if something had kept them awake most of the night after the previous day's hard work. Others were carrying out similar visitations at the respective abodes of the two Eamonns. So, within minutes we were well and truly lodged in a large basement cell at Victoria barracks. They had gone to some trouble before our arrival, arranging a special court and preparing charges which claimed that we had broken the order imposing a ban on processions and meetings in the scheduled area, i.e. Duke Street. Some hours after all this legal business we were escorted onto the footpath outside. We had been legally processed, being "remanded on bail to Derry Petty Sessions on October 21st by the Resident Magistrate, Mr J. M. Shearer, on bail."

Derry was in uproar since the Duke Street assaults. The night before had witnessed yet more baton charges as crowds were attacked in William Street. There were running battles with the police in Little James Street and in all about twenty were treated in hospital. Two were detained, a young boy and a policeman. The sound of breaking glass and the scream of the crowds echoed throughout this working class area until the crowds finally dispersed about 3.30am on that Sunday morning.

Later that same day trouble again flared in The Diamond area, the spot from which the civil rights marchers had been banned the previous day. Widespread violence occurred again after tea-time as the evening began. Large numbers of riot squad police with shields were deployed at Butcher Gate, an entry point to the old city and The Diamond which stands at its centre. Some 800 young people engaged the police at nearby Fahan Street and water cannon were again in action in an attempt to dampen down the situation in the Lecky Road. Other ancient gates were sealed off by the RUC. Shortly the fighting intensified as the main crowd grew to over 1000, many using steel rods, bricks and bottles to defend themselves. Timber barricades were constructed on Sackville Street in an effort to stop the police advances into the Bogside. Water cannon were used to smash another barricade in Rossville Street followed by a strong force of well-equipped police who were showered with stones. Petrol bombs appeared for the first time, mainly reserved for hurling at RUC Land Rovers. Over a dozen youths were treated in hospital. One newspaper reporter wrote: "blood-stained youths being led from the battle area were a common sight."

Meanwhile, Home Affairs Minister Willie Craig was seeing Reds who had dared to come from under their beds, and talked endlessly about the "pink IRA", (a change, some noted, from seeing pink elephants). This was the strangest of all his Vatican-inspired papist plots which linked the Communist Parties of Ireland and Britain, their supposed Trotskyite fellow-travellers, the Chief-of-Staff of the IRA, whom he claimed was at Duke Street, and any number of fantasies for the world media. The alleged IRA chief had been in Dublin, at least 150 miles away, and his main concern, according to those pressmen who met him, was to get his car properly repaired. For Craig, anything and everything was to blame except the real cause of discontent and protest – lack of proper housing, electoral gerrymandering plus sectarian practices and planning in the spheres of employment and economic development. These claims were all deemed to be irrelevant and false, and not to be considered for foreign reportage. We received descriptions of his every mood-swing, often within hours, for some journalists who met him would meet some of us later that night or next day and talk freely of their encounters with the 'hard man of Unionism'.

Banner headlines on October 8th showed that Westminister could no longer afford to ignore N. Ireland, discussion of which was a major taboo on the floor of the House of Commons. The *Derry Journal* of that Tuesday morning spoke of 'Dramatic development as city assesses cost of week-end disturbances – WILSON CALLS O'NEILL FOR TALKS ON DERRY SITUATION – Callaghan asked for full report.' Its front-page also carried the story that "trouble flared up on Sunday in The Diamond and last night when a crowd of about 100 young people threw up a barricade at the foot of Fahan Street and threw petrol bombs at police Land Rovers patrolling the area." It was now clear that the people had not run home from Duke Street and forgotten all about their demands for civil rights as the Unionist elite had hoped. A few column inches away, the same mayor of Derry, councillor William Beatty, who turned both a deaf ear and a blind eye to the homeless, got another headline. He had reluctantly agreed to meet the press, but "the press were not allowed to ask questions when he faced them in the Guildhall council chamber yesterday." He merely wished to emphasise the present and future economic development plans for Derry and the North West. He then delivered an appeal calling for an end to the unrest to the assembled newspaper, radio and television representatives from many parts of Britain and Ireland. Despite his original ban on them, reporters tried to ask questions. When asked by one reporter if his plans for the future dealt with electoral reform, "the mayor waved his hand and did not reply. When another reporter asked if the mayor was reluctant to answer questions because he represented only 30 per cent of the citizens, the mayor again raised his hand and signalled that the interview was over."

On the afternoon of October 9th three thousand students at Queen's University in Belfast, both Catholic and Protestant, decided to march in protest against police brutality in Derry. On the morning after the march, a mass meeting of students decided to establish a new organisation, People's Democracy. PD, which was to become the socialist wing of the civil rights movement, believed in direct action and warned that the Catholic middle class would try to sell out the civil rights struggle.

The City Hotel, on the evening of October 9th, became the venue for an unadvertised meeting, the origin of which is still surrounded in some mystery a quarter of a century later. It had not been called after any formal meeting or as a result of any agreed strategy on the part of the original organisers of the banned Duke Street demonstration. It was supposed to be merely a gathering of concerned citizens to discuss the local situation, as far as I was led to believe. Certainly at least two individuals are suspected of secretly lowering the drawbridge to admit others into a leadership role. The real facts are unclear however as to who actually made these arrangements in the few days following the march. The end result was the creation of the more broadly-based Derry Citizens' Action Committee (DCAC). At some point during the general discussion, which I deliberately did not attend, Eamonn McCann, who until then presided, left the assembly abruptly, declaring that he refused to accept membership of the new body. This shows clearly that the radicals had no agreed strategy on the way forward, and had become disorientated in the immediate aftermath of the dramatic march. McCann went public and castigated this development as "the kiss of death for the developing radical movement in Derry". The 'substantial citizens' whom he felt had jumped adroitly on the bandwagon, he painted as "middle class, middle aged, and middle of the road gentlemen". I was instinctively against any broadening of the original committee and had believed that the October 9th event was to be a useless debating exercise in which some pillars of society would merely warn against taking dangerous roads before retiring to the bar for a G&T to arrange their next golf-outing, or discuss their last package holiday.

That night I had surprising reports by phone that at least three prominent pro-civil rights Protestants, one a solicitor, had readily accepted membership and that all the remaining original organisers were prepared to give the new creation the benefit of the doubt. It was interesting that these included other members of the Londonderry Labour Party, of which McCann was the most prominent member. It clearly was not a total take-over and would not have worked if such a step had been attempted. I decided not to be a hurler on the ditch, or a purist in the wilderness and so joined the DCAC by invitation at its second meeting. I later became its education officer and honorary secretary. Most of the new arrivals in the aftermath of the march had played a role in the development of bodies such as the Credit Union or, like the Protestant solicitor Claude Wilton had been active in liberal politics, or had a track record of activity in related areas. They were part of the predominant reaction in Derry which was one of shock at state violence. They were disturbed at the scale of violence unleashed against the very victims of political, economic and social injustice. Even peaceful protest was forbidden in the city centre and, like the majority of Derry citizens, they felt further angered and diminished by such restrictions.

Elected to membership of the DCAC and subsequently elected as officers were Ivan Cooper (chair), John Hume (vice chair), Michael Canavan (secretary), James Doherty (treasurer), Campbell Austin (press officer who resigned at an early stage), Paul Grace (chief steward), Patrick L. Doherty (subsequently chief steward), John Patton (subsequently press officer), Finnbarr O'Doherty (subsequently education officer), Claude Wilton, William Kelsall, William Breslin, Brendan Hinds, Eamonn Melaugh, Dermot McClenaghan and John White. The last five named, and myself had been on the original organising committee of the October 5th demonstration.

The DCAC decided to develop a gradual programme of action both to build support and to explain the necessity for such action. Its activity was to prove crucial to winning long-awaited reforms. It was to remain in existence until shortly after the dramatic events of August 1969. Recorded minutes of meetings ceased after May 30th, around the same time as a meeting with the Prime Minister at Stormont Castle was being finalised. The homeless revolt now became absorbed into what had emerged as a mass movement, and its spearhead locally was primarily the DCAC. Against this back-cloth of dramatic mass demonstrations for a fuller package of reform, the single-issue of housing and homelessness was to remain high on the agitational agenda, as the DHAC maintained both its independence and identity.

During October the DCAC had opened offices at William Street to take statements from all those injured by police action during the October 5th demo. I assisted in the collection of this vital documentation which would in time reveal to the world the full extent of that state-sponsored brutality. The real figure of those injured at the Duke Street march was in the region of 88 people, most of whom did not go to hospital fearing arrest. A statement released by the same hospital authorities alleged that "only minimum action was used by the police."

The DCAC decided to organise a public meeting in the Guildhall Square on Saturday 19th. Its first press release called for restraint and promised to place a programme of action before the public: "The Committee is confident that its composition presents a strong hope for real change in our city. We guarantee a programme of positive action to achieve a united city where all men are equal." Prior to the sit-down, Campbell Austin, its press secretary and a leading Unionist business-man, resigned. He opposed such tactics and viewed sitting down in Guildhall Square as being "too militant". I wrote in my diary, "perhaps he prefers the Croppies to lie down."

The protest of October 19th was advertised as a 'sit-down' to signify to the authorities, and a watching world, the peaceful intent of the organisers and their supporters. Liberal, Labour and Conservative party HQs were requested to send observers. First-aid groups, St John Ambulance and Knights of Malta agreed to attend the sit-down. 400-500 stewards were recruited 'to control the rally', each being given an armband and coming under the control of Paul Grace, the chief steward. On the day, some 5,000 attended in spite of acute tension throughout the city. Each speaker delivered an analysis of one particular cause of discontent and linked these to the specific demands for reform. I spoke on the Special Powers Act and the denial of basic freedoms. Others on the panel addressed such topics as the lack of adequate housing, the demand for One Man – One Vote, the need for industrial development, the desire for boundary extension and community relations. The police kept their distance but sealed off Derry's walls with tenders and heavily armed reinforcements were stationed in side streets. The well attended protest, which had opened with a rendition of 'We Shall Overcome', closed without incident. The committee, local press and local observers noted the excellent performance of stewards and the public, and so it became clear that conflict could be avoided if the RUC continued to keep their distance and respected the basic rights of assembly and freedom of speech.

On October 21st, the DCAC decided to present a report to the public at Derry Guildhall at the end of the month and not to open negotiations with the authorities at that juncture. It was also agreed that all fifteen members of the committee would lead a linked-arms march on Saturday November 2nd, at 3pm. The route would be from the Waterside railway station to The Diamond via Duke Street, Craigavon Bridge, and Carlisle Road. At The Diamond it was intended to read the Declaration of Human Rights. The RUC were notified of the committee's intentions and it was decided that no other activity would be held prior to November 2nd.

On October 26th the committee issued a statement which invited the public to line the footpaths and assemble at The Diamond. The intention was that only the committee were to march in the middle of the road, three abreast. If the police attacked it was decided to offer no resistance, and if further progress became impossible the DCAC members would sit down and invite the public to do likewise. On the same day a peaceful march along the fourteen miles of road from Strabane to Derry was attacked at the village of Bready and later at Magheramason by some 400 loyalist counter-demonstrators. Banners were snatched and all eleven marchers were injured. Two were hospitalised. Only seven reached Guildhall Square to deliver their letter to the mayor.

The DCAC began attracting considerable assistance from the Northern Ireland Society of Labour Lawyers, (NISLL) which also provided observers at all mass demonstrations organised by the DCAC. The NISLL team was engaged with the DCAC in preparing documentation and preparing defence briefs. It was with some relief that this distinguished body, in a face to face meeting, agreed that they would undertake the defence of Eamonn McCann, Eamonn Melaugh and myself. We were due to eventually appear in court on charges relating to the organising of the parade on October 5th. We stressed that we would be making no apologies and that every effort must be made to highlight the social and economic conditions that took us on the road to Duke Street in the first instance. Such a stance, we were informed, might carry a high cost, which we felt would be well worth it to alert the world to the realities of life here. We were told that the defence team would be led by Martin McBirney QC, paradoxically the senior Crown prosecutor for Belfast, and that he would be assisted by a team of barristers and solicitors from the NISLL. We had no doubt that the outside world was watching. The committee frequently received requests for interviews from the foreign media. Derry-born Moira Hegarty O'Scannlain, based in San Francisco, was a welcome visitor. She conveyed fraternal greetings from Citizens for Irish Justice, an organisation which was established after the October 5th demo. Solidarity messages were also brought from several other bodies which spoke of contact being made with U Thant, Secretary General of the United Nations, Irish and British Ambassadors to the UN, President Johnson, Queen Elizabeth and Harold Wilson.

By the end of October there were unprecedented scenes at the monthly meeting of Derry Corporation. The chant of "Civil Rights" echoed through the Guildhall. There was an 'invasion' of the council chamber by people in the public gallery, one of whom occupied the mayor's chair, which the mayor had vacated during one of two adjournments of the meeting; a brief struggle between two Unionist members and nationalist Alderman Hegarty when the latter tried to wrest the chairmanship from the mayor; a sit-down in the corridor outside the council chamber and the calling of the police to clear the public gallery.

The spark this time was the refusal of the Unionist majority on the council to receive a Derry Labour Party deputation at the meeting to discuss the housing situation in the city. Some fifty people, including DHAC members, crowded the small public gallery. At the outset of the meeting, as the town clerk (Mr R. H. Henderson) was starting the business on the agenda, all the nationalist members immediately rose and shouted "Civil Rights!" The majority of them had been anywhere else other than Duke Street on October 5th, but then this was politics, as Gerry Fitt would have put it. We in the gallery joined in the chant.

When this finished Alderman Hegarty, amid applause and before the business could continue, began a lengthy address to all present. The applause began after his first few lines: "Mr Beatty, we can never again address as 'Mr Mayor' any individual who is a representative of minority rule in this city – not that very many more, if any, minority mayors will occupy the mayoral chair in this Guildhall".

The scene was like something I remembered from the films on the French Revolution, and the atmosphere was truly electric and exhilarating. The masses were speaking, and their former undemocratic masters were now in the public dock. Other councillors such as James Redmond Doherty spoke, with the mayor interrupting him saying they must proceed with the agenda. He failed to see what the real business of the day was all about and that his agenda was now totally insignificant. He insisted, "We are going to do the business of the meeting." Some of the public shouted, "Impostor" and another voice was heard, "Send for your riot squad". As the tension mounted, the mayor and Unionist councillors went out of the council chamber after declaring an adjournment. Immediately some of the protesters occupied the seats left vacant as they had threatened to if the Unionists left the chamber. The chairman of the DHAC, Eamonn Melaugh, occupied the mayoral chair, and said: "I ask you citizens of Derry, do you approve of a crash programme of 2,000 houses?" There were cries of "Yes". He then asked,

"Do we extend the boundary? – Yes". Before leaving the chair he commented, "This is democracy!"

A teach-in was now being conducted in the public gallery, with references being made to a married couple with three children, who lived in a room 9 feet by 10 feet with several of the protesters saying there were many families in similar situations. The mayor returned. He wanted the proceedings to go into committee. There was opposition from the nationalist benches and slow hand claps from the public. As the Unionist majority voted to adjourn, a struggle ensued between Alderman Hegarty and the mayor over who should occupy the chair. Other Unionists went to the mayor's aid, as he resisted being pushed out of it. A great deal happened during the unfolding drama which did not end even when the RUC arrived. The public gallery was gradually vacated without a struggle. The Unionists then returned yet again to begin to discuss their original agenda 'in committee' – an hour and three-quarters after they first assembled. The protesters gathered on the steps leading to the assembly hall and continued their teach-in which broke up peacefully at 2pm. The Unionists however finally agreed to receive the Labour deputation to discuss housing and other social problems, at a special meeting the following Friday.

November opened with a request from the RUC to meet DCAC officials on the morning of the proposed march at 9.45 am. This was agreed to. The police would be told that we planned to march regardless of yet another supposed counter-demonstration, this time by a group using the name 'Loyal Sons'. They would also be told that the committee planned a mass march on November 16th, and that invited organisations would include all branches of NICRA. November 2nd dawned, again with some apprehension. A change in the order of the marchers was agreed. The DCAC executive would be in front to deal at once with difficulties that might arise. Labour Lawyers would be on hand to offer advice as difficulty was expected at Ferryquay Gate. Frank Curran's book graphically described the events of that day:

> On 2nd November, watched by a silent disciplined crowd of about 4,000,
> the DCAC marched the route proscribed on 5th October. The object was
> to establish the right of a non-Orange march to parade peacefully
> through the streets. The police remained inactive, and threats by Ian
> Paisley's side-kick, Major Ronald Bunting, that the march would be
> resisted, led to nothing more than isolated scuffles at the Derry end of
> Craigavon Bridge. The Committee emphasised that the march again

proved that public demonstrations need not lead to disorder as long as
they were properly organised and police and hard-line Unionists made no
moves to oppose them.   *('Derry, Countdown to Disaster', p90)*

We had reached The Diamond and had our speeches. The Human Rights Declaration was read by an 11 year-old boy as a symbol of the future we wished to create for the next generation. The DCAC, following the end of the march, issued a brief but highly significant statement: "The universal right of any citizen to march through Derry, so unjustly denied us on 5th October, has been clearly established."

On Armistice Day, November 11th, more summonses were delivered to the two Eamonns and myself relating to defying the ban at the October 5th demo. The net was widened that day to include some forty-three others with Ivan Cooper and Eddie McAteer MP, the nationalist opposition leader at Stormont, being added to the list.

Two days later an emergency meeting of the Committee was called for 5.30pm in the office of Cllr James Doherty to discuss the position arising out of the ban imposed by Home Affairs Minister William Craig on all processions and meetings within Derry Walls. It was decided to send a telegram to the British Prime Minister asking for protection to enjoy fundamental human rights. A press statement was issued clarifying the situation. It was also agreed to carry on with preparations for the planned march of November 16th. In case of dawn arrests it was decided that each member would appoint a personal delegate to guarantee that the march would go ahead.

The day before the mass demonstration there was a major turn-out of stewards. It was decided that appointed members of the DCAC would attempt a symbolic confrontation with the police at the barriers, which would be erected because of the minister's ban. The executive would not decide until the eleventh hour between Duke Street or Spencer Road as an appropriate route. History was about to repeat itself, this time as farce. A press statement was released expressing the wish that only those intent on a peaceful non-provocative march would be welcome in the city next day. An attempt at mediation with the authorities by all the main local churchmen had proven unsuccessful. The two Bishops, Dr Farren and Dr Tyndall announced that special vigils for peace would be held at the Protestant and Catholic cathedrals from 10pm until 6am. Civil rights leaders and supporters, with clergy and faithful of different religions, participated throughout the eight hours intercession. This march had caused acute tension. It would later be seen as a high point or watershed that occurred on Day 42 of the 'Fifty-Day Revolution'.

The Committee decided at 1pm to stop 30 yards from police barriers while Ivan Cooper addressed the police. At all costs the majority were determined to avoid a full frontal confrontation. A minority on the left, which included myself, felt that one way or another Craig's ban would have to be broken and soon. The mood of the people was equally militant. If the police refused us permission to march further, then four committee men would be instructed to climb over the barriers and symbolically break the law. A meeting would be held on the bridge and the speakers would be Messrs, I. Cooper, J. Hume, F. O'Doherty, Jas Doherty and C. Wilton. The body of the march was to be kept informed by loudspeakers mounted on a lorry. Then we would disperse, peace-fully. At least that was the plan!

That Saturday afternoon a huge gathering, estimated at 20,000 people, assembled at Duke Street to march over the October 5th route, led by DCAC members. The vast concourse was blocked by the double line of barricades erected at Carlisle Circus, behind which a large force of police stood guard, leaving only the route to Guildhall Square via John Street open. RUC County Inspector Paul Kerr was placed in command of these visibly terrified state forces. He reminded us all of Craig's ban on demos inside the Walls. Ivan Cooper and John Hume then called on the police to allow the marchers to proceed but senior police officers refused to comply. At this point Michael Canavan, Johnny White, Dermot McClenaghan and Willie Breslin put the next stage of the pre-arranged plan into operation.

They symbolically broke the law as they climbed over the first line of barricades without opposition but were repulsed at the second barr-icade by the police. Regrouping they charged forward again, eventually breaching the barricade line.

Some would later claim that "the marchers, satisfied that the symbolic breach had made the civil rights case, then streamed down John Street towards Guildhall Square." This was not what I remember or recorded at the time. I was speaking on the platform while the symbolic breach was being made and explaining what was happening to the crowd. Many were extremely angry, heckling, booing and calling, in no uncertain terms and in the most floral of language to "Move forwards", "Sweep the pigs aside, we have the numbers now!"

Loyalists around a Union Jack tossed stones at the demonstrators from the RUC side of the barriers yet the police remained inactive. Stewards led marchers to John Street away from the planned route. Large numbers of marchers broke away and advanced up Bridge Street towards Ferryquay Gate and the walled city. There were fierce clashes with right wing loyalists which lasted half an hour before police and their Orange allies were swept aside by sheer force of numbers. Derry's Diamond was thus occupied and the police made for the shelter of Shipquay Street. At 4.45pm the RUC commanders ordered a complete retreat.

At The Diamond a few of the speakers endeavoured to claim that by our presence there we had won a great victory, insofar as "the right of Derry people to march and meet peacefully in their own city had now been re-established." This was a gross distortion I felt, for if the original plan had been carried out we would have dispersed and gone home, thus kow-towing to Craig and his cohorts. I saw neither victory nor defeat as we had yet to walk from A to B along the original route without interference. Some DCAC members verbalised their concerns about what line I might take, as my turn came to speak. I began my address by saying, "Like James Doherty, I too come from a long line of butchers, but I do not believe in mincing my words." As far as the left was concerned Craig's ban had been broken only by default and other methods would have to be agreed and implemented at a conclave before appearing at court.

On the morning of November 18th the October 5th defendants duly appeared at the Bishop Street court. This day would show what positive working class action could achieve, over and above sporadic street battles with well-equipped police. Our youth, regardless of the numbers involved, suffered proportionally greater injuries than their uniformed opposition, who had the full backing of a ruthless state machine. Craig personified the Orange psyche when he banned civil rights demonstrators from within or on Derry's Walls. This was their Orange Mecca, and collectively Unionism was still suffering from the siege mentality of the 1600s. Once a curfew bell tolled the knell of parting day for native Catholics: they had to be out of the city walls after it rang. Now instead of a bell there stood the sectarian RUC who manned its ancient Gates, as if King James had just returned again from France to claim his English crown. We were not a foreign army of invaders and the very Walls themselves had been built from our demolished forts, abbeys, public buildings and dwelling places more than three centuries before. The

Derry working class would do something that even King James and his European allies never did. We would push aside its latter-day defenders, and seize the city and the world headlines. We would physically demand the right to simply walk on our own Irish streets, when and where we choose, and in a non-sectarian fashion to boot.

This was the day for the proletariat to assert its rights. It would mark a high point in the history of Derry's working class. It would be a day that would long be remembered by thousands of chanting demonstrators who would tell their children and grandchildren how with bare hands they answered the call and made their way from their respective places of employment, towards the banned area, not knowing what savage repression awaited them. This series of demonstrations had been sparked off by the hearing of prosecutions against 46 of us who took part in the banned march of October 5th. Some fifty people were refused entry to the public gallery of the courthouse, as the cases were being heard. Only the defendants, witnesses and members of the press were allowed by the police to enter the court building. The principle of 'Justice being seen to be done' was of course again being denied to the general public. That is not to say that we ever got justice with a packed gallery. The crowd outside swelled to about 100 and when the hearing inside was about fifteen minutes in progress a group of about 50 tried to get into the building. They were physically blocked by police at the main doorway.

There was an appeal by the DCAC's chief steward, Paul Grace, a member of the local Labour Party, who told the crowd they could only damage the cases being heard inside by demonstrating. Councillor James Doherty, who was on the Duke Street march, also spoke. After some tough talking with the police, a senior RUC officer relented and allowed about a dozen relatives of the defendants to enter the court. Outside, four members of the DHAC arrived carrying placards, one of which read 'Justice on Trial Today', and proceeded to parade in front of the courthouse and police until the hearings ended.

Some of the defendants, including Gerry Fitt MP and Ivan Cooper, seemed quite content to be lifted shoulder-high and be carried down Bishop Street, through The Diamond and Shipquay Street to Guildhall Square. The crowd had grown to around 300 and was singing 'We Shall Overcome'. By taking such action, technically inside the Walls, the ban was actually being defied. The police, geared up to stop 'intruders' coming from outside the Walls, were caught on the hop yet again! This march from the courthouse was a good humoured affair after the lively court proceedings, yet it ended in a short clash with police on the steps of the Guildhall, just outside the Walls. The RUC never seemed to understand that their every inept move was giving even greater fuel to our own publicity engine, and that when Derry shouted, now, the world was really listening. Again they would let their bigoted hearts rule their empty heads. Fitt, and we other leading defendants, merely wished to address the gathering of supporters and to use the Guildhall entrance steps as a platform. Officials rushed to shut the iron gates as they believed we had come to enter the building – which even foreign journalists were quick to point out was our 'City Hall', built by ourselves, the rate-paying citizens!

Not content with the gates being shut, the police assaulted people as they moved through the crowd. Fitt, Cooper, Agnew and a few other defendants addressed the meeting and appealed for calm, in the certain belief that the police were trying to provoke the general public yet again. The crowd did not go home as advised, but rather marched off again, retracing their steps through Shipquay Gate to The Diamond, and down Butcher Street – the long way home for most of them. Craig's ban had been broken twice within less than an hour, and all his Queen's water cannon and all his own RUC 'A' men and 'B' men couldn't put his stupid ban together again. Down along the docks the natives were feeling equally restless. About half-an-hour after the Guildhall crowd had taken their illegal route home, some 400 dockers left their work, leaving the tools of their trade behind them. They staged a march through the city centre to their union headquarters. As they pushed past police they sang 'We Shall Overcome' – now a song of which almost everybody knew at least the first verse and chorus. They told the press that they were protesting against recent police assaults at the Guildhall. They marched down Ferryquay Street and Orchard Street where they staged a sit-down in the middle of the road.

At their request their branch secretary, George Hamil, undertook to send telegrams to Captain O'Neill and Harold Wilson, the Prime Ministers of N. Ireland and Britain. The march leader was a Phil Doherty, who said he hoped that these messages might assist in righting wrongs which had been done in Derry, especially those affecting Derry dockers and their families and to highlight and protest against the incidents which occurred at the Guildhall. The dockers were addressed by Vincent Coyle and John Hume. The police withdrew some distance after the latter told their officers, "we can keep the peace ourselves. We don't need you." After their branch secretary promised that he would send the telegrams and urged them to return to work immediately, the dockers formed up and marched back to the docks behind the Guildhall, via Newmarket Street, Ferryquay Street and Shipquay Street. On their way they sang civil rights songs and chanted "SS-RUC!" At the dockside meeting, John Hume, later to be a founder member of the SDLP, a Westminister and Euro MP, congratulated the dockers on their spontaneous action and said that it was action like that which showed the world that their spirit was the spirit of Derry.

Some of the leading defendants went to the City Hotel after the court proceedings. Others, including myself, retired to the upstairs lounge of the Grandstand after the dockers' protests. We felt that the ban must not only be broken, but be broken by as many people as possible and as often as possible, to make it a complete nonsense and to discredit Craig politically so that he would never try the same tactic ever again. The meeting, which included some of the original Duke Street march organisers, agreed that we would break up and approach trade unionists and workers directly throughout the city. My task was to approach shop stewards at a shirt factory immediately opposite the bar. This was the area in which I was born and had spent all my teenage years so I was ideal for the purpose, and was already well-known as a civil rights activist. I addressed the shirt factory employees from a workbench. The speech was short and the reaction was sweet; they merely wished to know what time they should down tools for an hour of protest. With their wholehearted support I visited other factories in the Queens Street-Strand Road area. Sometimes I didn't even have to speak at all. The word was being spread throughout the city, and had reached a few shirt factories before me.

At the agreed time, shortly before 3pm, about 1,000 factory workers left their work benches in about half a dozen factories and organised a march, again through the banned centre of the city. One of those pictured leading one of the marches was a determined-looking Nelly McDonnell who had fought her own lonely fight some months previously in Harvey Street. The sight of defiant, chanting and singing female workers seemed to strike more terror into the police than the dockers had done earlier, which I noted as highly interesting at the time.

There was a wonderful feeling of class solidarity as the streets became filled with waves of human protesters whose fine voices sang of a new tomorrow, their feet marching ever forward, and along the way the police were pushed aside while being bombarded with chants such as "Gestapo!" and "The workers, united, shall never be defeated!" Everyone pressed on until they reached The Diamond where they were addressed by several leaders of the civil rights movement. Messrs. Hume and Cooper, who had remained in the city centre area since the dockers' demo, were the most prominent speakers. Cooper told them: "On behalf of the DCAC I congratulate you. Well done. The women of Derry have for years borne the brunt of unemployment and bad housing conditions."

May Duggar, a spokesperson for her fellow workers, made it plain that they were marching to defy the minister's ban on marches through the walls of Derry, and would be back again if he imposed another similar ban. Eamonn McCann told the marchers: "You have shown today that Mr Craig's ban is not worth the paper it's written on. The factory girls of Derry have walked all over Herr Craig's ban." After listening to other speakers, the women then re-formed and marched through Shipquay Gate yet again and down Strand Road, chanting even louder as they passed the main RUC station, before their chosen dispersal point at Great James Street. Workers from other occupations also staged their own marches that same afternoon, and everywhere there was a tangible sense of intense jubilation.

That night, pro-Craig loyalist males from the nearby Fountain Street district attacked women shirt workers as they emerged from the Cerdic Factory at the junction of Abercorn Road and Wapping Lane at about 11pm. This hostile element had targeted the factory because it was the nearest to them and possibly because it was also managed by Ivan Cooper, a Protestant who was now a leading civil rights figure. Bottles were thrown and women employees screamed and tried to get away from the onslaught. Two of the workers required hospital treatment. An historic day was thus ended, and the famous Walls of the Maiden City had been well and truly breached.

November 19th witnessed yet another historic meeting in Derry Guildhall, called by the DCAC to present a report to the public on completion of their month's brief. An attendance of over 5,000 people was recorded, packing the main hall, minor hall, corridors, stairs and other areas, as well as overspilling into Guildhall Square. Internal and external public address systems were set up beforehand. A minute's silence was observed as a mark of respect on the death of Mr White of Leenan Gardens, the father of one of the October 5th march organisers.

It was decided by the meeting that the Committee would be re-elected by acclaim: that their term of office would continue until full civil rights were won. Names recommended for inclusion were Mrs McKimm and Eamonn McCann. Among the Committee members who addressed the large gathering were Messrs B. Kelsall, F. O'Doherty, D. McClenahan, B. Hynes, J. Hume, P.L. Doherty, J. Patton and P. Grace. From the audience the following spoke: Messrs E. McCann*, Alderman J. Hegarty, M. O'Leary, G. 'the Bird' Doherty, J. Campbell, J. Carlin, S. Keenan†, and women speakers included Breege McFadden and the journalist and women's rights campaigner Nell McCafferty. A collection was taken up from the audience to defray campaign expenses.

Day 47 of the 'Fifty Day Revolution' ended with yet another meeting of the Committee. There was some concern expressed at the fact that demonstrations were now becoming 'spontaneous'. The Labour Lawyer, Vincent Hanna proposed that a statement be issued to the press urging no demonstrations unless approved by the DCAC. This was carried and reflected the tension that was being created between the 'moderates' and the 'radicals', as hints of the events about to unfold would result in a battle for hearts and minds. The Committee also expressed concern that several stewards were reporting victimisation at their places of work and promised that this would be investigated and should be deplored. Talk by stewards of organising a boycott of firms which were responsible for victimisation was generally frowned upon. At this November 21st meeting I was elected as education officer, and this position was linked to a project to recruit qualified personnel to work on an independent Development Plan, e.g. to produce our own second Wilson report.

---

* *Eamonn McCann at this meeting was full of praise for the DCAC. He commented thus: "I have had many disagreements with members of the Committee, but last Saturday when I looked at 15,000 to 20,000 Derry people off their knees and ready to fight for their rights, I realised we had a lot to be thankful for in having this committee."*

† *Sean Keenan also spoke from the floor of the Guildhall that evening. Almost a quarter of a century later the front page of 'Saoirse - Irish Freedom' would report thus: "As we went to press we learned the sad news of the death on March 3rd of Sean Keenan, of Derry, Honorary Vice-President of Republican Sinn Fein, in Altnagelvin Hospital, in his native city. He was 78. Ruairi O'Bradaigh, President, Republican Sinn Fein, paid an immediate tribute to Sean Keenan: 'He endured a lifetime of struggle for the freedom of Ireland. Sean was interned for a total of 16 years in the Six Counties yet never stood in a court in his life'."('Saoirse', No. 71, March, 1993).*

The real significance of the 'spontaneous' demonstrations of dockers and shirt factory workers in Derry may in time be fully revealed. Radicals believe that Craig's position was seriously undermined, which was the aim of the demos in the first place. When official documents are released after the '30-year rule' we may yet find that these were the straw that broke the Stormont camel's back and resulted in speeding up the limited reform package which followed on Day 48 of 'the revolution'.

On that day, councillors responded to an urgent invitation from Prime Minister O'Neill to come and see him at Stormont. It is significant that Craig was not in attendance, suggesting that the 'hard man' had been turned into a man of straw behind the Unionist screens. The PM's message was delivered without much ceremony, quite abruptly and at some speed. In short, the Londonderry Corporation and the Rural Council were to be suspended and a commission appointed to carry out the Derry Development Plan. This was the first of several bombshells that would be dropped on local hard-liners from their own leaders on high. The asylum-keepers were getting their marching orders at long last. They effectively lost control of Derry City and beyond on November 22nd 1968. They were naturally devastated, while the civil rights movement was elated.

Next day the reform proposals of the Stormont government were examined in detail and the Committee's attitude was defined under six headings:

1. it was decided to welcome the introduction of a recognised points system in housing;

2. to welcome in principle the appointment of a Parliamentary Commissioner (Ombudsman) but to urge the extension of his powers to local government affairs;

3. to welcome in principle the idea of a Development Commission for the implementation of the Area Plan and await further details. The Committee hoped that it would be set up in such an objective manner that it would be sufficiently strong and well qualified to ensure houses for the homeless and jobs for the jobless speedily;

4. to welcome the abolition of the company vote;

5. to declare that on the Special Powers issue the PM's statement was too vague. It seemed to indicate that the government was not willing to amend a subsequent statement by Home Affairs minister Mr Craig. This strongly indicated that there was in fact no change. This apparent conflict makes it difficult to place confidence in the govern-

ment's intentions in this whole situation, when confidence is of the essence. We believe that the Special Powers Act should be abolished and that existing legislation is adequate without it;

6. furthermore, we resent the total failure of the government to face up to the central issue, democratic rule in this city, because this is the root cause of the present unrest in this area. We pledge to continue the struggle until this is achieved.

These points were released to the press and the statement concluded:

We congratulate the people of this historic city on what has been
achieved to date and ask them to continue to exercise restraint. We feel
confident of their support when we call for it again.

The last lines hinted strongly that the DCAC was prepared to give O'Neill and the Stormont government some breathing space. The DHAC began to talk of 'a truce' and issued a statement calling for the pressure to be maintained. Radicals elsewhere had their own agendas which included breaking any alleged truce with Stormont. The PD began to work out a strategy whereby such a break could be achieved.

Against this background the November meeting of the Londonderry Corporation was certainly not to be missed. For all anti-Unionists it was a jubilant affair with the public gallery filled with people who had come to gloat at the Corporation's latest misfortunes and see how the poor souls would be taking it all. Every human emotion surfaced during its death throes. There were only three statutory meetings left to hold. November was therefore the first night of the wake for one-party minority Unionist rule in Derry. We opened our vocal chords and began to sing 'Auld Lang Syne' as the meeting drew to a close. The choice of song was both appropriate and symbolic. In short, it heralded a victory for common sense achieved by the common people. It was they, and they alone who had endured and won!

December 1968 was indeed a busy month. The first issue of *Reality*, published in early 1969, (to coincide with the arrival of the PD march) reported under the heading, 'Guildhall Hunger Strike':

On December 9th, six homeless families took up abode in Derry
Guildhall and refused to move. These included Mr & Mrs Ambrose
Moore; Mr Dan Kerr, 16 Donegal Place; Mrs Gorman, 55 Spencer Road;
Mr P Bradley, 269 Bishop St; Mr & Mrs Healey, 30c Dove Gardens;
Mrs Bridget Bond, 40 Foyle Road; Mr Tony Doherty (student) and
a 15 year-old machinist Patrick Hutton. The latter three are active

members of the DHAC and joined Mr Moore in a hunger-strike
lasting 35 hours.

After meetings with the mayor and the standing committee of the Corporation the Moore family received temporary accommodation. A promise was made that the cases of the other families would be considered and the sit-in ended, agreeing to leave the Guildhall at 5.45pm, after spending the night there. On December 14th, members of the DHAC were back, this time picketing "against the lack of proper sanitary facilities in hundreds of Rachman-owned flats in the city. Placards included such slogans as 'Homes not Slums', 'Bring Sanity to the Sanitary Department', and called for the dismissal of the city Executive Sanitary Officer, Mr Drayson." The DHAC objected to the fact that this official refused to close down slums and was "against the Housing Trust closing down good houses in the redevelopment area". It must be said that Drayson and some other officials, over recent years, had expressed many concerns in their departmental reports, but these were subjected to the now traditional deaf ear and blind eye approach of the city's ruling elite. They also were victims of the reactionary cocktail called discrimination that, by its very nature, required blending housing allocation with sectarian electoral politics.

On Monday 16th, with the full team of Labour Lawyers in place, including its chief spokesperson Vincent Hanna, a new twist in the October 5th saga was enacted at Derry Petty Sessions. Our cases, and those linked to some 87 other summonses, were granted an adjournment for five months. This amounted to an amnesty for the large number of civil rights protesters threatened with prosecutions in Derry, Armagh, Dungannon and Strabane. Also included in this gesture were those Unionists who had resorted to violence against peaceful marchers, during counter-demonstrations and other incidents. The police, faithful servants of the Unionist regime, were of course not excluded by the terms laid down by Barry Shaw, QC, senior counsel for the prosecution. Conveniently, there was no mention by Shaw of actions taken against the police during his legal address to that court.

OCCUPATION

On the housing front, it became clear that promises made during the December 9th protest were not carried through. In the closing days of 1968 the DHAC was to return to the Guildhall for an even longer and more dramatic occupation.

Eamonn McCann's book 'War and an Irish Town', captures the militancy of the homeless, yet does not convey the details in full. The Unionists were back to their old ways. At their monthly meeting they voted down proposals to build houses on the Glen Road. All hell broke loose as the homeless continually interrupted proceedings to relate their own cases in public. Even this was considered not militant enough by the DHAC executive and the mood of the people was reflected by subsequent occurrences at this meeting. A man who had endured as much as most, Daniel Harkin, walked to the mayor's ornate chair and told him: "I was born and reared in this city and have three children. One is suffering from pneumonia. Can I hold you to account if anything happens to my children?" Councillor Beatty showed no compassion and retorted that Mr Harkin "was not entitled to be here". Stephen Canavan shouted that he had been walking around Derry for the previous two weeks looking for one room. He continued: "I cannot walk the streets for one more night. My wife and I buried our six week-old child two weeks ago. Others may die." The mayor refused to suspend standing orders so that the people might be heard. As the meeting drew to a close and they packed up their papers and prepared to leave, the homeless rushed to every door and stopped the mayor and councillors from leaving. They were effectively forced back to their seats and made to listen to a concise list of complaints. Eventually the mayor agreed to provide temporary accommodation for the Canavans the next day.

The mayor had made no promise to assist the remaining families, who were equally desperate. He had effectively made a token gesture to escape from the immediate pressure upon himself and his Unionist colleagues. Human compassion was never a factor that surfaced in such dealings with this or previous mayors. Holding onto power was always their first, and it seems, only priority, regardless of the negative conseq-uences for Derry citizens as a whole and in particular the homeless.

Daniel Harkin and other families decided to stay put. Blankets, foodstuffs and other necessities were immediately required to make life more bearable, and a democratic structure for internal decision-making was also a priority. The gravity of our situation began to sink in, and the potential threat from the police and far-right elements was in the back of all the adults' minds. It was decided that as this was intended to be a protracted 'live-in' as opposed to a short-term 'sit-in' as before, there was a need to elect our own city council. This would be something which would be primarily functional as opposed to being merely symbolic. The debate raged about titles, with the majority supporting the view that we elect our own mayor. Our mayor would remain in office until everyone got suitable temporary accommodation, pending the availability of permanent houses, and of course would be elected by the citizens and their offspring who were present.

We had hardly caught our breath before the election began. Even the children were demanding a say in the process, and it was agreed that they too should have the franchise. The nominations were listed, and no deposit was necessary. I was elected 'The Mayor', with no opposition as no one else was nominated. Without ceremony I took the mayoral hot seat. Two others were elected to assist the new first citizen. These were Tony O'Doherty (no relative I hasten to add), distribution manager of *Reality*, who would handle public relations, and Leo Coyle who would beg or borrow provisions and finance. 'War and an Irish Town' relates that 'the mayor' and his officials issued "a number of decrees", the first of which was that we would hold out until our collective demands were met, if not evicted beforehand.

With police at the front and the rear of the Guildhall, food and milk were smuggled into the council chamber via the ladies toilets, one floor above. Exit from and re-entry to the Guildhall initially involved shinning down the broad drain-pipes conveniently placed near the windows. Ladies tights, men's ties and other items of clothing formed a rope, and foodstuffs were more than willingly supplied by staff at the City Hotel, then managed by a gentleman from Kerry. Brendan Duddy who ran a fish restaurant and Doherty's bakery, who had premises in William Street, provided their products on a complimentary basis when food and money ran extremely short. The protest had caught the airwaves and the imagination. Two days after the 'live-in' began, twelve adults and five children arrived looking for accommodation, and were admitted.

Local and foreign media personnel were told that the police would effectively starve out those participating in the occupation. However, in addition to the support outlined above, ordinary citizens passing the large iron gates at the front of the Guildhall often threw in loose change they could spare, some handed in bottles of milk and even fish and chips to be shared around. This was particularly true over the festive New Year period, when small bottles of wine, cans of lager and Guinness passed through the gates during the evening hours. One particular brand of wine, made in racist South Africa but very popular among some local 'connoisseurs', was banned from the council chamber, much to the disgust of one specific inhabitant who spoke very highly of its warming qualities before bedtime. (The same gentleman would gladly have had it for breakfast as well alongside his cornflakes and milk. He further claimed that it had even been recommended by his family doctor, in a bid to increase his chances of acquiring this potent beverage). It has been claimed that the famous Derry-born playwright Brian Friel was so inspired by our occupation that he wrote his acclaimed play, 'Freedom of the City'.

Some recall that at the first meeting on the day of occupation a proposal was tabled by our resident 'connoisseur' which recommended improved communications with the outside world. In support of the motion he said he could only endure the forthcoming ordeal if a television set was installed so that he could watch the Wednesday evening programme, 'Match of the Day'. They relate that it was duly supplied by Deery's of Butcher Street and that the indoor aerial was hung over the city's coat-of-arms which formed the apex of the mayor's chair. The effect of having TV was to create other unforeseen difficulties. This same male occupant, after watching Buddhist monks burning themselves in protest at US policy in Vietnam, threatened to adopt a similar course of action during visits by members of the media. This 'human torch' threat caused both embarrassment and genuine concern. The incoming mail increased in volume as a result. Some packages, containing small tubes of lighter fuel, the striking edges of match-boxes and their contents, bore sectarian messages from local loyalists who requested that this "Fenian bastard" give ample notification as to the day and time when such would occur outside on Guildhall Square. Many occupants feared for the mental state of their fellow protester, who continued to insist that he was deadly serious. He withdrew his threat when all present agreed that none would accept alternative accommodation, until he and his family had first been satisfactorily housed. As a bonus he was permitted another brand of wine from a non-racist state, with certain restrictive strings attached.

The council chamber also became a place for political debate as the DHAC struggled to work out a response to the limited reforms of PM Capt. O'Neill. Whatever position we took then would have a bearing on how we related to other organisations. Our members would be expected to push DHAC policies within their respective organisations. We came out in favour of the radical perspective, to press on for one person – one vote and give no respite whatsoever to either the PM or the one-party Stormont regime. This meant that I and a few others would go on the Belfast to Derry march organised by the People's Democracy.

We hoped to join it at Antrim town and on arrival we were surrounded by a group of young Paisleyites. They barracked us to state our religion. As they pushed us forward they indicated that they wished to continue their interviews in a laneway some distance ahead on the main street. Ironically the RUC spared us from an unknown fate. I managed to escape from our interrogators by dashing into a group of policemen who suddenly came around a corner. I explained the situation quickly and indicated who my friends were. They formed a circle around us, then bundled us into a van and with little comment drove us safely to a community hall where the marchers were beginning to eat and arrange space for bedding down that night.

A few nights later, the barriers erected by the homeless in the Guildhall proved effective, even against another aroused Paisleyite faction. The 'Big Man', Paisley himself, and Major Bunting had graced the city with their presence. This was on the night before the PD march was due to arrive in Derry. The march was attracting increased support as PM O'Neill, during a speech on TV failed to promise 'One Man – One Vote'. This four-day march, which started on January 1st and snaked along the ninety-mile route from Belfast (being frequently harassed by loyalists), was to be a major political turning-point. Loyalists yet again failed to understand, or simply rejected, the PD message. They had tried to link their militancy with a clear appeal to Protestant workers. They were not just for more jobs and houses for Catholics and less for Protestants – they wanted better conditions for *all* workers. Later, in Armagh, the message would get through as Protestant and Catholic tenants participated in joint action. Loyalist opposition, however, assisted the radical agenda insofar as the march could not be ignored by the world media, and the participation of B Specials along the route did much to reveal the sectarian nature of the Stormont regime and the nature of its 'policing'. The loyalists unwittingly turned the march into a victory for the left-wing of the civil rights movement. Every step forward was earning more column inches while loyalists did all in their power to scatter the marchers and stop the demo from ever reaching Derry. The prime leader of the PD march, Michael Farrell, later recorded the historical details in his work, 'Northern Ireland: The Orange State', (Pluto Press 1976). In this he remarked:

The march would be the acid test of the government's intentions. Either

the government would face up to the extreme right of its own Unionist
Party and protect the march from the "harassing and hindering"
immediately threatened by Major Bunting, or it would be exposed as
impotent in the face of sectarian thuggery, and Westminster would be
forced to intervene, re-opening the whole Irish question for the first time
in 50 years. The march was modelled on the Selma-Montgomery march
in Alabama in 1966, which had exposed the racist thuggery of America's
deep-South and forced the US government into major reforms.   (p249)

The occupation of the Guildhall had become highly symbolic for both the loyalist and the reformist movements. Tension was rising with each hour of the march as people listened to radio or TV announcements on progress (or lack of it). Those inside the Guildhall knew that they were the physical embodiment of that symbolism, which they faced with an intense mixture of both pride and fear. Some children were evacuated, other parents were determined to keep their families intact, come hell, high water, or Ian Paisley.

The anger of the Unionist establishment at the occupation of the Guildhall might well have figured in the reasoning of the Rev. Ian Kyle Paisley and Major Bunting, when they chose that specific time and place to arouse their followers for action next day. Above the heads of the homeless that distinctive thundering voice of Paisley echoed throughout the Guildhall. Just below, the children and adults entertained themselves with all manner of activity including telling bed-time stories, some involving a 'Big Bad Wolf' which seemed most appropriate in retrospect.

The plans to attack the People's Democracy students' march were outlined at this Paisleyite rally. However, the exact chosen place of attack was to remain a secret, possibly because those below their platform could hear almost every word. In the hall were a few pro-civil rights Protestants who updated radical leaders on the proceedings.

Outside the council chamber major rioting erupted that night in Guildhall Square. As the meeting ended Paisleyite factions emerged armed with parts of broken chairs. They seemed foolishly anxious to engage in hand-to-hand battles with nationalist youths, as if to present them with a major test of their supposed commitment to those non-violent policies advocated by the civil rights leadership. Such were not always practised by the rank and file, when faced with deliberate physical abuse. The scene was dramatically illuminated by Major Bunting's car, which burned fiercely after being torched. This caused great joy outside on the part of nationalists, but great concern to those still in occupation. The homeless families could not tell if the council chamber itself was the intended target, or what faction was doing what. Meanwhile, McCann and myself had left the march, and while Paisley was inside, we were outside calling on the people to join the march as plans were being made to attack it the next day. We stood on railings outside a nearby bank and managed to keep erect by wrapping one arm around a post which bore a sign for traffic which read, appropriately, 'Strictly No Waiting'. What happened after the Paisley-Bunting rally at the Guildhall is graphically described in Michael Farrell's authoritative work:

> On 4th January the march set out from Claudy swelled by several
> hundred supporters who had come out from Derry. A few miles out from
> the village they were halted again and then allowed to proceed with a
> warning that there might be some stone-throwing ahead. A bit suspicious
> of the RUC's sudden willingness to let them march they went ahead. At
> Burntollet Bridge several hundred loyalists hurled rocks and bottles and
> then charged, armed with clubs and iron bars. It was an ambush. The
> spot was well chosen, the loyalists were on a height and dozens of
> marchers were driven off the road and into the river Faughan, some
> quite badly injured." (p250)

Farrell continues:

> There is no doubt that it was a trap. The RUC knew an ambush had
> been prepared. Heaps of stones had been collected the night before and
> crowds of cudgel-wielding men had been gathering since early morning
> while RUC men stood among them laughing and chatting. During the
> ambush some of the RUC joined in and attacked the marchers too. After
> the attack they made no attempt to arrest any of the loyalists. I
> remember going back to the bridge and finding RUC and ambushers
> sitting about relaxing. It later turned out that nearly a hundred of the
> ambush party were off-duty B Specials. (p251)

The occupiers of the Guildhall, now mainly women and children, listened with some apprehension to the incoming news. Eventually the battered bulk of the marchers trudged on to Derry, meeting further opposition at Irish Street estate on the edge of the Waterside, and from a quarry on high ground on Spencer Road. In sight was Craigavon Bridge, from which the Guildhall is clearly visible. As the sound of the march drew near, women and children pressed their faces against the closed wrought-iron gates at the front of the Guildhall. The adults were fully conscious that they were witnessing history in the making. Children joined in the cheering. All felt a wish to be part of this rapturous welcome that was afforded the marchers from a huge crowd that had gathered in Guildhall Square. Assistance for the injured became an urgent priority as they trudged into the Square. Several were led by the arms or carried into the City Hotel, now the unofficial HQ of the DCAC. To its front doors several ambulances came and went, taking the more serious casualties, several of them young people, to hospital. Others shrugged off their injuries and stood with dried blood matting their hair and covering their clothes, grateful to be alive as they acknowledged the cheers of the crowds. Among these were the late Frank Gogarty, a Belfast dentist who was the tireless chairman and veteran of NICRA, and his two teenage sons who had taken turns carrying a leading banner, which they still doggedly held onto. An emotional series of speeches were delivered from a platform outside the council chamber. Amid the subsequent singing it was clear to all that the militant wing of the civil rights movement was visibly badly bruised and bloodied but certainly far from bowed. Firmly clenched fists were dramatically raised as 'The Internationale' echoed off Derry's ancient Walls, possibly for the first time ever, but certainly not the last. From this date forward I heard no more from my DCAC colleagues about 'let's give O'Neill a chance'.

As darkness fell anxiety mounted, both inside the council chamber and without. The *Sunday Press* of January 5th, carried the headline: 'TERROR OF DERRY – 200 injured as march ends in riot'. The report elaborated:

> Riots escalated again in Derry after the end of the four-day, 80 mile, civil rights march from Belfast. The casualty total was quoted as high as 200, with at least 89 people treated in Altnagelvin Hospital just outside Derry. Others had their injuries attended to elsewhere.
>
> Two armoured water cannon were in action in the city just before nightfall and there were repeated baton charges in Strand Road and around Butcher's Gate. People fled in all directions as the water cannon, with their klaxon horns blaring, roared through the centre of the city.
>
> After the civil rights demonstration broke up in Guildhall Square, and despite appeals by stewards to disperse and go home, sections of the crowd tried to reach The Diamond, which is within the ancient city walls.
>
> Major Ronald Bunting, leader of the Loyal Citizens of Ulster, had announced that he had planned to stage a trooping of the colours – the red, white and blue Union Jack. Hundreds of people of all ages tried to

storm their way through several approaches to The Diamond, but police
tenders blocked the archways around the city walls. Rumour was rife,
and when it was reported that one of the water cannons had knocked
down a young person without stopping, the crowd became incensed and
four baton charges by the RUC were made in the area of Strand Road
and William Street.

State terror and collaboration by police with reactionary forces was always a reality for those who challenged the status quo. It was with some dread therefore that the barricades inside the council chamber were further reinforced. News was trickling through that sections of the police were drinking openly as they roamed the city centre streets. Several male radicals shinned their way up the drain-pipes to lend physical support to those who remained determined to maintain their occupation of Derry Guildhall. That night, however, police attention was to be focused elsewhere. RUC Reserve personnel, many clearly drunk and apparently furious that the marchers had got through to Guildhall Square in spite of intense loyalist opposition, ran amok in the Catholic St Columb's Wells. These 'officers of the law' further disgraced themselves by breaking windows and smashing down doors in order to viciously baton and kick anyone in sight. The nationalist people were naturally outraged, and proceeded to build dozens of barricades. Thereby Free Derry was born out of necessity, rather than radical design. The RUC were kept out of the area for a week. Meanwhile, local residents, with the assistance of the Derry Citizens' Action Committee, chartered a plane to fly to Westminster to relate their individual tales of state repression to scores of Members of Parliament and a shocked British media. For the majority it was to be their first ever air flight, and quite an occasion for all involved. As Farrell was to conclude:

Burntollet was the turning point for the civil rights movement. They would
accept no further promises or excuses, they wanted civil rights –
especially 'One Man, One Vote' – immediately.   *(p252)*

My *Morning Star*, formerly the *Daily Worker*, of January 8th was full of news about a major demonstration outside Marlborough House, London, as the Commonwealth Premiers' Conference began. The cartoon by 'Eccles' seemed highly appropriate. It showed a black leader in his traditional dress and headgear standing on a footpath in London. He is staring at demonstrators who are approaching carrying banners that read 'End the Discrimination', 'Ulster Police state', 'Civil Rights for Derry', and 'One Man – One Vote'. The puzzled visitor, looking at this sea of white faces, asks: "And which part of the Commonwealth are you from?"

Those who played a part in the unfolding saga of those times were later to write the following letter, which duly appeared in the columns of *Reality*:

Dear Editor,

We the undersigned, former residents of the council chamber, wish to express our sincere thanks for the marvellous support given to us during our 7-week squat-in at Derry Guildhall. We will remain eternally grateful to the Derry Housing Action Committee for their moral, financial and active support. If it had not been for such support we have no doubt that we would still reside at our former addresses and live in the horrific conditions prevailing there. On behalf of ourselves and our children, we wish also to include in this thanks those members of the general public who displayed such great kindness. May God reward you all for the interest shown in our plight.

Joe Clarke	Daniel Harkin	Nellie Gorman
Formerly of 92 Bishop St	f/o 40 Carlisle Rd	f/o 55 Spencer Rd
Bridget Bond	John Parke	F. Crookeshank,
f/o Foyle Rd	(f/o address unstated)	f/o Spencer Rd
Joe Nash	Willie Healy	John Gillespie
f/o 15 Orchard St	f/o 30c Dove Gardens	f/o The Diamond
Dan Kerr	Patsy Bradley	
f/o Donegal Place	f/o Bishop St	

Reality editorialised:

The action of the above families proves beyond a shadow of a doubt that direct action brings results. The local authorities have been forced to re-open sound dwellings to accommodate these families, and would never have done so but for militant action. The DHAC were not demanding new homes, but rather we did demand that the Corporation allocate to each a better abode in which each family could bring up their children in a healthy environment. There is no doubt that our policy is the correct one and has brought the desired results.

The number of families during the period under review that squatted into dwellings must run into several hundred. Clearly, the people were so desperate that no property was sacred, and the better the standard of property the more likely it was to be occupied. It was therefore poetic justice that government property proved the most attractive.

Some 29 families occupied houses owned by the MoD at Clooney

Park South between May 10th and 13th. Some 34 married quarters, formerly used by Royal Navy HQ personnel stationed at 'Sea Eagle' became surplus to Ministry of Defence requirements. Understandably, the homeless of Derry found such 'surplus' overtly disgusting and promptly took steps to remedy their situation. One squatter told pressmen, "it is probably the first time in their lives that some of these children have played on grass," pointing to children playing on swings and see-saws on the green in front of the houses. "It's lovely here," was the comment of another squatter.

Nine months later the *Derry Journal* (February 27th 1970) reported that the MoD was trying to get these back, this time for their soldiers. The local Labour Party, who backed the squatters throughout, warned the MoD against any plans for evictions, adding:

> Squatting was a reaction to the lack of houses which, with
> unemployment, was one of the twin fountain-heads of discontent in
> Derry. Now the Ministry is threatening to evict squatters to make way for
> the troops who came in as a result of that discontent boiling over.
> Homeless families in Derry have a moral right to enter and occupy
> vacant dwellings. Certainly they have more right to houses in Derry than
> soldiers of the British army. The Ministry is inviting trouble if it attempts
> to evict the residents of Clooney Park.

Before then, however, the Unionist PM, Captain O'Neill, was considering house-moving options himself. Apparently he "could no longer abide the snapping dogs at Stormont, and on 4th February 1969 an election was called for the twenty-fourth day of the month", writes former DCAC member, Dr Raymond McClean, in his book, 'The Road to Bloody Sunday' (Ward River Press, 1983). This same source remarks:

> Two days after the election, Brian Morton took over as Chairman of the
> new Londonderry Development Commission, the body which had been
> appointed to replace the disbanded Londonderry Corporation. Mr Morton
> stated that the housing situation in Derry was "frightening", and he
> immediately instituted a massive building programme, ironically enough
> in the old North Ward of the gerrymandered corporation area, and out
> into Carnhill and Shantallow. The old city boundary, and with it the
> gerrymander, had gone for ever. (p65)

The DHAC had played a major role in the downfall of the old corporation, and in later times its demands for a points system in the allocation of houses became accepted everyday practice when the Northern Ireland Housing Executive (NIHE) became a major force for progressive change throughout the Six Counties. DHAC demands, once viewed as 'radical', were soon being considered as reasonable, fair and routine, even by government-appointed agency boards. DHAC's emphasis now seemed to change to one of playing an overtly political role in opposition to the Unionist regime, as if the sequential victories of its first year of existence had removed one sectarian nine-pin after another. Only one was left to tackle, the stubborn one-party system, Stormont itself.

The *Londonderry Sentinel*, a pro-Unionist newspaper, watched the antics of the DHAC from its infancy and gave prominent coverage to the organisation's last major public meeting. I suspect some of its journalists sympathised with the socialist cause. Its reports reflect a grass-roots movement with women, such as the late Bridget Bond, its backbone. Another outstanding woman was the dedicated Labourite, the late Kathy Harkin, who did much to aid the cause of the homeless and established Derry's first women's shelter, thereby exposing a problem that was all too often kept concealed. Newspaper reports too often quoted men as being the prime spokespersons as if the women were dumb or dim or had nothing constructive to say. However, the *Sentinel* reporters on this occasion were not slow to pick up the higher stakes being played for by the more radical elements, of both genders.

The *Sentinel* report of the last major rally reflects an intense disgust and distrust by the radical elements, of the more 'moderate' Catholic forces who were, some argued, seeking 'respectability' with their sights firmly fixed on walking along those 'corridors of power'. For the left, street politics still had a role to play, whereas those who sought parliamentary positions felt that such had outlived its usefulness, in more ways than one. The latter were viewed as turning their backs on public agitation, which seemed to belong to the pre-election past. Events would show that this was wishful thinking. At times of crisis working class militants would return instinctively to the streets, seeing this as the only forum available in which to express their own frustrations based on social alienation. The left feared that it was being marginalised, yet while the poorer people still yearned for jobs and proper housing the radical forces still had a positive role to play. In an election in early 1969 the PD confronted both nationalist and Unionist politicians and managed to poll 25,000 votes. At the border during a Belfast to Dublin march PD showed its contempt of the Southern state by presenting Irish gardai (police) with banned novels by Edna O'Brien.

The better-off Catholic middle class, did not share the same sense of urgency, simply because they had jobs, a roof over their head that they could call their own, a car and annual holiday etc. These economic disparities created a real gulf in terms of respective aspirations and tactics. This class division did not seem to be widely understood at the time, as various elements charted separate courses for themselves, within, or outside, the official civil rights movement. The Catholic middle class had its own agenda, of that there can be no dispute. It was never articulated in public, because this would be disadvantageous to them. This class, the 'Castle Catholics', had been kept out of the running of the Northern statelet, ninety-three per cent of the top civil servants being Protestants.

The Catholic middle class hoped to use the mass movement to prise open positions for themselves. Radicals, they felt, wanted to 'go too far', and we felt that the struggle had not gone far enough. We knew that they wanted to get their slice of the cake by reaching an accommodation with the Unionist regime, a regime which many on the left, were determined to see overthrown. (This left did not include the then leadership of the republican movement in Dublin which sought the mere 'democratisation of Stormont'). What stood in the 'moderates' way was the militancy of the working class ghettos and the opposition of the Paisleyites. This meant that they could never fully reach an accommodation with the liberal wing of Unionism, personified by Terence O'Neill. By the end of 1968 the moderates who had taken control of NICRA called a 'truce'. The Burntollet march, and the stance maintained by radicals then and subsequently, must be viewed in this context if one is to understand the extra-parliamentary strategy. The leaders of the PD, local Labour Party, and the DHAC knew only too well why it was essential to continue with street politics.

The *Londonderry Sentinel* reported the last DHAC rally under the dramatic headline 'Rising Against Public Order Bill' as follows:

> When Derry Housing Action Committee staged a meeting in the Guildhall Square on St Patrick's Night, the first anniversary of the Committee's formation, Finnbarr O'Doherty, secretary of the Committee, referred to the proposed passing of the Public Order Bill, and said: "I am speaking personally, but I say that no Derryman or woman worth their salt would lie down when the hour comes. We will rise with our comrades, in Belfast, in Toombridge and in Antrim, and throughout the North; we shall say to the Fascists of Stormont, 'You know what to do

with your Public Order Amendment Bill'." The audience of about 200
turned up in bitterly cold weather.

Mr O'Doherty, who is honorary secretary of the Housing Action
Committee, and the new honorary secretary of the Derry Citizens' Action
Committee, said the road which lay ahead of them would make the past
events look like a garden party. After referring to people who supported
the pro-O'Neill candidate he said: "To hell with any form of Unionism, be
it extreme Unionism or liberal Unionism."

NO GHETTOS

"We will see the day when there will be no ghettos and when
Protestant and Catholic will sit round one table, and live in the same
estate. The reason for bigotry is that it comes from segregation, founded
on fear that one section will over-ride the wishes of another," he said.

Mr O'Doherty also said that in the so-called Republic of Ireland the
government would pass the Criminal Justice Bill which was "every bit as
vicious as the Special Powers Act", and he added: "We will continue to
fight the RUC batons and water-cannons and the new Minister of Home
Affairs who is no better than Craig."

SEND OVER TROOPS

Mr Eamonn Melaugh, a founder-member of the Housing Action
Committee, said he had a message for the British Prime Minister:

"Mr Wilson, get ready to send over the troops to Ulster because you
are going to need them. The RUC with all their arms could not keep us
off the streets and Captain O'Neill with a piece of white paper at
Stormont will not either."

LIKE PRIZE FIGHT

After declaring that "one in every 10 families in Derry didn't have a
roof over their heads," Mr Melaugh said: "It is sad that housing in Derry
is like a prize in a prize fight – if you are not prepared to get off your
knees you will spend seven or eight years in a filthy hovel, paying an
exorbitant rent to some of these pillars of the churches. They call
themselves Christians, but they are Christians for an hour on Sundays
and blood-sucking vampires for the rest of the week.".

Mr MeLaugh later said that the Rachmans were to be found in the
Catholic Church as well as in other churches. He said:

"We have had our demonstrations for civil rights, and I have shouted
'One Man, One Vote' until I was sick, sore and tired. We shout 'One
Family, One House' and we demand the right to work without
discrimination. If the government refuses to fulfil its duties, it is our duty

to get out on the streets. Power in this day lies between the pavements on each side of the streets."

BACK TO THE STREETS

Bernadette Devlin, unsuccessful candidate in South Derry, said:

"We have been off the streets for a long time and we have not had anything yet. The People's Democracy will be back on the streets at the end of this month, particularly because of the new Public Order Act. This is the most important thing to date. Some say "Give O'Neill time". What did he do? He gave us the Public Order Bill. We will have better homes. We have the right to live in decent houses, and if we can't live in one he is not going to live in a big house – the people of Derry will come and live there. There's a big building at Stormont – far be it from me to suggest that the people of Derry should live there for a while." Miss Devlin also said, "Get off your knees. Start marching. Nobody has the right or the capabilities to stop you."

The *Sentinel* report showed that there was a battle for hearts and minds still in progress. It gave more than a hint of the fall-out that would follow in the coming few months, which some viewed then as merely exaggerated scare-mongering. The PD was quickly becoming the spearhead of working class action on the streets and was in the thick of the internal wranglings in the civil rights movement. However, the Dublin-based republican leadership was totally out of touch with grass-roots opinion in the North, and even its own rank and file in their attitude towards Stormont. Eventually, even the British Conservatives realised that this particular rotten barrel was beyond refurbishment via reform, as they imposed direct rule without consulting any Irish tendency, left, right or centre. This proved that these six counties were nothing more grand than a small colonial outpost north-west of London, and were therefore treated in true imperialist fashion. In early 1969, however, the rainbow coalition that was the civil rights movement began to separate into its various coloured strands. A series of verbal battles would eventually reach many an editor's desk, in terms of claim and counter-claim. Almost every area of the Six Counties would be affected. The unexpected decision by Captain Terence O'Neill to call a snap election for February 24th threw the movement into a fit of activity, that created both confusion and discord. One could argue that the movement would never fully recover.

This poll had put the cat among the proverbial pigeons in the Orange Tory camp as well. Everywhere people seemed to rush to their respective banners and corners to mobilise their forces for the contest. Talk about "unity and speaking with one voice" within the civil rights movement was pure farce disguising tragedy, as the basic demands became a means rather than an end. This snap electoral contest almost tore the DCAC and other reformist bodies asunder. There were plenty now who uttered Brendan Behan's dreaded word "split". Even the closely-knit Derry republicans couldn't agree among themselves, as the group in the city selected me, well in advance of Nomination Day (February 13th), to go forward on the abstentionist ticket. A forgotten branch in Coleraine insisted that the convention was undemocratic as they were not in attendance. I argued that they were correct and that a more democratic convention should be assembled and that it should select another candidate. None was called as others must have realised, as I did at the time, that the republican vote was small last time round in 1966. Also we stood no chance of having a candidate elected, especially as our policy was to abstain from any partitionist assembly. The voter-in-the-street, who had sympathy for the republican cause, nevertheless wanted to be represented, and wished their cat let loose among the Stormont pigeons. I decided that the radical vote would be torn apart, and that the effect would be to drive another nail into what looked like being the coffin for the civil rights movement. Before eleven months had passed the republican movement itself would be split asunder, in every part of Ireland and overseas.

Now, even the 'moderates' were not at all moderate as they tossed abuse at each other. Letters and phone calls I received from Nationalist Party supporters told of the civil rights movement's colours, black and white, "being used in a most opportunist and incorrect fashion locally to gain public office". Our colours, like the movement, were never supposed to be linked to the specific politics of any group or individual. On this issue the DCAC honorary treasurer, Cllr James Doherty also wrote to me, this being his expected resignation after expressing his feelings to an internal meeting. The entire committee noted his letter with genuine regret, and I recorded such in the minute book following its March 14th meeting. His position was filled by Michael Canavan, a local bookmaker and businessman.

The Londonderry Labour Party threw its hat into the ring also, with, I felt, little chance of success. Thirteen 'rebel', i.e. hard-line, Unionist MPs declared they would challenge PM O'Neill, whom they considered a moderate. These included a man few civil righters would be voting for,

Albert Anderson, who had had a disastrous five year term as the city's mayor. A local pro-O'Neill group set up a caravan outside the Guildhall to collect signatures for a petition which called on Anderson "to withdraw his name from the demand for a change of Prime Minster and support Captain O'Neill." Before ending their activities at 9pm on Monday February 3rd, they had collected some 3,000 signatures, which showed that many local Unionists would have supported at least some basic reforms.

March was to witness this process of fragmentation, but this time it would be 'on the left', as the alleged 'Trots' and 'Stalinists' made claim and counter-claim. It was a most interesting month indeed, being on the left, as events rolled on. The real question now was would the movement survive, and had we all got batoned, soaked, arrested, and charged merely to put a handful of fresh faces into one parliament or other? At least that's what people were asking on the street corners or when out for a few pints. The *Sunday Press* of March 16th was reporting: 'Civil Rights take over is denied – 'Nonsense' says Farrell'. It was to present the flavour of the period thus:

> Two men who spearheaded the civil rights campaign have resigned their offices from the Derry Citizens' Action Committee while four leading officers of the Six County Civil Rights Association resigned over "political infiltration".
>
> The first two are Ivan Cooper, Mid-Derry's new Member of Parliament, and John Hume, MP for Foyle. They resigned "because they did not want to mix politics with civil rights activities", a committee statement said yesterday.
>
> The statement added that they tendered their resignations to forestall any confusion in the public mind between their political positions and the non-political aims of the civil rights movement. But both men will remain members of the Committee, the statement added.
>
> The other four are: Mr John McAnearney, Secretary, Civil Rights Council; Mr Fred Heatley, Treasurer. and founder-member; Miss Betty Sinclair, former chairman; and Dr Raymond Shearer. Miss Sinclair is Sec. of the Six-County Communist Party.
>
> One of their complaints is there was "a take-over bid of the movement under way by a political party." Allegations of a take-over by the People's Democracy, a semi-student group based at Queen's University, Belfast, were hotly denied by Mr Michael Farrell, a leading member.

It was "absolute nonsense," he said. And he declared that the two
People's Democracy members on the 18-man executive were
"democratically elected at the Civil Rights Association annual meeting."

Miss Sinclair said last night: "The decision taken to jointly sponsor a
demonstration in Belfast on March 29th with the People's Democracy,
which is an admittedly political movement, was not in keeping with the
aims of the Civil Rights constitution. The position is that PD policy is
geared to appeal to activities that would seem to be left-wing and which,
I think are adventurous."

All this should be put into a realistic context, however. No mass movement can appear on the scene without endeavouring to make an institutional impact after an initial period of mass action and extra-parliamentary protests, be that movement of the right, left or centre. There was bound to be friction as people adjusted to changing political circumstances and fortunes. Only history can judge if parliamentary participation had an overall beneficial effect in the struggle to achieve all the original demands of the movement – demands which a quarter of a century later have yet to be fulfilled with regard to discrimination in employment.

In this context the internal conflicts were understandable. The inevitable clash of personalities and loyalties proved a strain on individuals and organisations alike, and even now ill-feeling still lingers. The local political scene had changed beyond recognition in the first quarter of 1969. In effect, the death-knell of the old Nationalist Party had been sounded and its eventual wake and burial could not be too far off. People would remember that they had (one week before October 5th) publicly refused to take part in the march, as a party, in their own Irish city. Some of its leaders had, however, been quite happy to jet off to walk in parades in the far-off USA. Some of its leaders did not desert the common people and their struggles, and had been to Dungannon and arrived at Duke Street. They included Eddie McAteer and Cllr James Doherty, who were sampling police truncheons when I was in short-pants. They had in the period 1950-2 attempted to organise peaceful marches, including one on St Patrick's Day, when the green was soaked with the red of native blood from many battered heads.

One sight, of a nationalist Alderman standing in the council chamber pointing his finger amid Orange and Green Tory encouragement, would not be easily erased from the memory of the homeless. This 'city father' claimed that the DHAC chairman, Matt O'Leary was "a card-carrying member of the Communist Party" and that somehow the rest of us were all dupes. This unwarranted and untrue comment had caused O'Leary to hastily call a press conference at which he resigned so as not to harm the struggle for homes. This he did against popular advice and without any internal pressure from the DHAC rank and file. The controversy hurt him and his immediate family deeply, as some editors unleashed their reporters on the scent of 'a good story'. Not all comrades were as sensitive as Matt. One press hound was to tell me of what happened when he and a few other journalists 'cornered' the quick-witted McCann. When asked if he was a "card carrying member of the Communist Party of Ireland", he simply shrugged his shoulders and told them that their editors should know that he had never been that far to the right. The interview ended with the press scratching their heads with their pencils as McCann entered the nearest pub for a well-deserved pint.

It was as if McCarthyism was well and truly alive in Derry's local council, and that even those who should have been defending the right of citizens to proper accommodation placed this priority below that of grabbing dubious headlines. Some obviously hoped that 'Red scares' might prevent class issues coming to the fore and at the same time drive a wedge into the ranks of the homeless protest movement. The issue became even clearer when the Londonderry Labour Party and other city organisations wholeheartedly supported the march and took part in it. Kevin Agnew, the civil rights lawyer and champion of the homeless put his pen to paper and asked in the columns of the *Journal*:

> What other Nationalists of importance, including the Corporation
> Nationalist members, took part in the march? Those who didn't ought to
> be ashamed of themselves; or perhaps they're not interested in civil rights
> for the working class in Derry (or, should I say the workless class).
>
> *(October 8th 1968)*

By the end of March 1969 the new faces at Stormont may have had an influence. Possibly 'Big Brother' at Whitehall had decided that N. Ireland was attracting too much global media attention. What was apparently unthinkable in early October 1968 was now there for all to see. National newspapers such as the *Sunday Press* (Dublin) had an historic page three pin-up photograph in their March 30th issue. The lens had captured the image of several lines of RUC constables leading a local civil rights demonstration the previous afternoon. Another picture worthy of pin-up status showed flag-waving Paisleyites taunting the marchers, but this time for a change they were kept at a respectable distance.

In time a points system was introduced for house allocation, and Unionist control of this sphere was seriously undermined as the civil rights demand for PR was finally conceded. Proportional representation, introduced into the electoral system in the early 1970s, was a body-blow to the one-party system that Stormont had been for some fifty years. The Derry Housing Action Committee lingered on in the midst of major social upheavals during the summer 'Orange Marching Season' of 1969. On the fringe of the Bogside the annual Orange march was attacked by bottles and stones tossed by nationalist youths. A whole community was now determined to stop such displays of Orange ascendancy on their very doorsteps, while they were being denied the right to march themselves in a city where they held a factual majority. Their militant action resulted in a joint attempt by the RUC and Paisleyites to invade the Bogside and teach its working class a lesson. A series of street battles lasting for almost three days ended with the British troops appearing on the fringe of the Bogside, "in support of the civil authority", i.e. Stormont. By that stage the RUC were well and truly exhausted. They took turns to sleep in some battle-free street or alleyway. Others were now being replaced by B Specials who put on masks and equipped themselves with pick-axe handles.

While several families and businesses were burnt out during 'The Battle of the Bogside', our counterparts in the Belfast Housing Action Committees faced a much more horrific task. During the months of July, August and September in that city, 1,820 families left their homes, 1,505 of whom were Catholics.

Gerry Adams' book, 'The Politics of Irish Freedom' (Brandon Books, Kerry, 1986) captures the times, and exposes the myth that the British 'came to protect the Catholics' (as if they had been absent before) from the extremes of the Stormont regime. He wrote:

> Arms were rushed up from the 26 Counties and barricades were
> strengthened to meet the continuing loyalist attacks. British troops took
> up position on the Falls Road, they did not intervene to take down
> barricades but neither did they intervene when loyalists burned down the
> whole of Catholic Bombay Street and a young Fianna* boy, Gerard
> McCauley, was killed trying to defend the street. As the RUC and loyalists

---

* Na Fianna Eireann, republican boy scouts. Set up in 1905, in opposition to Baden-Powell's ultra-patriotic organisation, by Countess Constance Markievicz, the first woman to be elected to Parliament in a British election

attacked Ardoyne, another Catholic street, Brookfield Street, was
burned down.   *(p33)*

Gerry Adams, like others involved in the early struggles against homelessness, was to be vaulted onto centre stage, and for almost two decades, in spite of several assassination attempts on his life, has remained the foremost spokesperson of the Provisional republican movement nationally. During those earlier struggles, even republicans were calling for the same rights as existed in Liverpool, London, Glasgow and Cardiff, arguing logically that "Stormont claims that we are British citizens, and must remain British citizens, so therefore let them grant us the same rights as those enjoyed by those who reside in Britain". Such carefully worded statements did not compromise long-term nationalist aspirations. Rather, they showed that the question of partition was not viewed as the central issue. Ulster Unionists conveniently ignored this fact. Instead they endeavoured, with a great degree of success, to sectarianise the civil rights campaign, in the minds of Protestant workers generally. Only a handful of Marxist intellectuals seemed to argue that there was a need to analyse the very nature of the state. Yet, even here there were those like Dr Roy Johnson, a leading figure in the Wolfe Tone Society, who argued, well into the 1970s, that N. Ireland could be democratised, from within. What was 'the State' and in whose interests did it operate? Was it capable of being moulded by popular pressure? Or was it a mechanism that had a built-in capacity to withstand potential innovation? The majority of activists, in retrospect, seem to be mere innocents abroad. They fought for what they felt was just and reasonable, without a fuller appreciation of the repressive capabilities of the State.

The actual revolutionary potential of reformist ideology within such a backward, sectarian and introverted statelet, was not fully understood by the bulk of leading activists. The fact that the mountainous mess in John Bull's backyard had been conveniently ignored by Westminster for generations was to lead to political eruptions of volcanic proportions resulting in streams of red lava that would flow without stop for at least one generation.

Adams was to write of the period after the early rumblings of that political volcano:

The situation had developed rapidly. The demands of the civil rights
movement had been demands for rights which were taken for granted in
western Europe and they were demands for rights which existed in the

*rest of the so-called United Kingdom. In retrospect they were, in
themselves, unremarkable, simple and moderate demands. Yet they had
evoked a ferocious response from the state and its supporters and the
consequence of that response had left the authority and stability of the
state in tatters. When I had first become involved in political action I had
asked myself what was so rebellious about asking for jobs; what was so
treasonable about demanding a decent home; what was so subversive
about seeking equal voting rights? I had received my answer,
as had we all.*   *(p34)*

Gerry Adams, former Member of Parliament for West Belfast, again
with the benefit of a now older and wiser head that provides us all with
the luxury of retrospection, presents a realistic analysis in the afore-
mentioned work:

*The civil rights movement had been looking for democratisation of the
state, but the state had made abundantly clear the fact that it would not
and could not implement democratic reforms. The movement had placed
its demands on the state; it had not demanded the abolition of the state,
nor a United Ireland. Now, however, with the reaction of the state and
the intervention of the British army, the constitutional question had
come to the fore and the whole existence of the Six County state
stood in question.*   *(p34)*

FOUR

Sunday, Bloody Sunday

January 30th 1972 in Derry witnessed a premeditated slaughter of peaceful civilian demonstrators at the hands of the British army's First Parachute Regiment. When the imperialist guns fell silent, thirteen marchers lay dead or dying, while seventeen others were seriously wounded. The British media told an unsuspecting world that their troopers had been fired upon, yet as the coffin lids were being nailed down amid a nation stopped by general strike and stunned by grief, not one British soldier had been treated for any injury received on that date.

Slowly the world began to realise that the truth will always out. That something very different from the version beamed across the globe by British radio and television transmitters, or the crude versions adopted by the lie machines of Fleet Street, had occurred on that historic date in the working class area known as the Bogside. Unlike our dead, the truth could not be buried under the clay but rather, like the blossoms on their graves, it burst forth from the soil to expose its reality to the full view of civilised humanity in the four corners of the earth.

The British, under the guise of an 'impartial inquiry' led by a former high-ranking imperialist army officer, and current Territorial Army officer, Lord Widgery, vainly endeavoured to pluck the flower of truth by all manner of distortion, omission and calumny. At all costs the British establishment and its lackeys within this artificial statelet, conscious of an international audience, adopted the stance of Pontius Pilate. As with this biblical figure, history will condemn in spite of public ablution.

The sun shone that day as over 25,000 peaceful demonstrators marched under the civil rights banner to protest against the arrests, torture and imprisonment of suspected opponents of the Stormont junta, without so much as a charge or a trial. This was the only way that working class people could express their abhorrence of government policy. The streets became their parliament, and their political desires were expressed in chants, the carrying of placards, or the singing of 'We Shall Overcome'. The power of the masses, which existed between the kerbstones of our streets and the ditches of our country roads, was a force that the British government was determined to crush. Like on so many other occasions, the British ruling elite could only respond to passive resistance on the part of a colonised people by the use of brutal state terror in the form of its standing army. On January 30th 1972, the city of Derry witnessed the latest organised massacre in the long and bloody history of the British Empire, which in previous times committed similar atrocities in Asia, Africa, the Americas, the sub-continent of India, and many other lands which were colonised, and over which its Butcher's Apron once triumphantly flew.

Before Widgery and the world, two sets of witnesses appeared. On the one hand, the 'soldiers' who had performed this dastardly deed, every one conflicting every other soldier's account. On the other, civilian witnesses who told a different story. They were unanimous and quite explicit that the army opened fire without provocation.

Any event in history cannot be fully understood unless we seek out the root cause – the chain of events leading up to such happenings. Our blood stained the pavements and barricades of Free Derry because of the fact that the minority within this artificial six county statelet had been denied their basic human rights since the inception of Stormont. Its establishment also had its roots planted in eight hundred years of British military, cultural and economic interference in our country. It was but a few years before Bloody Sunday that this minority began to demand equality in relation to votes, housing and employment, and had been met by frequent baton charges to drive the protest movement off the streets, the first such charge being in Derry on October 5th 1968. In the months that followed, serious rioting broke out all over this imposed statelet, as members of the RUC endeavoured to invade nationalist ghettos, as in April and August 1969, with the murder of Sammy Devenney at the hands of the police, the battles of the Bogside and of the Falls Road in Belfast. The nationalist communities took on a defensive role, and after the police force were driven back in a state of extreme physical and mental exhaustion, the British government sent in their troops "to aid the civilian authority", viz, the police and the Stormont junta. 'A House Divided', written by former British PM, Jim Callaghan, reveals that the Six County administration feared that after the defeat of their police force on the streets of Derry, the nationalist people would come out of their ghettos and take over the city. This was how he endeavoured to 'justify' his sending in their troops, which in reality had never left the six north-eastern counties – four of which, like Derry City, have nationalist majorities.

Sporadic rioting continued, but by the early summer of 1971 the British were content at the 'progress' being made. The RUC were once again patrolling almost all areas on foot, and the British army was little in evidence. By the beginning of July, however, a number of incidents had changed the local political scene very dramatically. The youth were once again on the streets resisting the powers-that-be, and a formerly quiescent Irish Republican Army were now in open armed conflict, and were steadily growing numerically and in terms of political influence. The prime reason for this new upsurge of militancy within the nationalist community was the unwarranted murders on July 8th of Seamus Cusack and Desmond Beattie in Derry by the forces of occupation. Such was the abhorrence of the working class communities at large that even the moderate middle-class leadership within the Social Democratic and Labour Party were forced by massive popular opinion to withdraw from the sham that was Stormont. If they had remained at this juncture, while still being able to attract mainly Catholic middle-class support, their political demise would have been certain, as grass-roots support in the working class areas would have vanished. Total rejection of the party would have been the verdict of the risen communities, believing that any clinging to power was for purely fiscal considerations.

By August 1971 the Stormont junta reverted to its age-old arsenal with the view to introducing its most repressive of weapons, so often used in the past with varying degrees of 'success', i.e. internment without charge or trial. It had been used in the Twenties, in the Thirties, in the Forties, in the Fifties and into the early Sixties, and was once again to be used in the Seventies rather than concede the basic demands of the nationalist communities. Unlike other more subtle regimes, Stormont had not learnt that the old methods used in former times do not always have the same results in new and changing situations. That a previously doubtful deterrent can in a different situation become a political catalyst for opponents, which in turn can produce a cataclysm – thereby having a boomerang effect.

On the morning of August 9th 1971, at approximately 4.30 am, young men from all over British-occupied Ireland were kidnapped from their beds by armed men, taken away and held as hostages, without charge or trial. Some were not so young, but all were nationalists. The pattern was not new. According to ex-internee John McGuffin, in his work 'Internment!' (published by Anvil Books, Co. Kerry in July 1973):

> At 6.45 am on 14th August 1969, 28 republicans were arrested and taken from their homes. As usual, no 'loyalist' extremists or gunmen were arrested. When the English Special Branch men arrived next month to sort out the RUC they asked for the files on all the "terrorists". They were handed records, mostly out-of-date, on the IRA. "What about the UVF?", they asked. "It doesn't exist", was the reply. "We have no records on loyalists." *(p84)*

The then Prime Minister of this sectarian statelet, Brian Arthur Deane Faulkner (now deceased), was an old hand at internment, having being responsible for its implementation in 1959, when Minister of Home Affairs. McGuffin relates:

> The Sunday Times 'Insight' team claim that "when he took over, the issue was not whether internment was to come, but when and on what scale." It is not surprising therefore, that on becoming the last PM of N. Ireland, he was to order the RUC Special Branch "to work with the Director of Military Intelligence at Lisburn in drawing up a list of those Catholics (sic) who should be interned".

McGuffin's research argues:

> The [British] army were unhappy. General Tuzo, the GOC in Northern Ireland since February 1971, consistently opposed internment, believing, rightly, as it turned out, that they could not get the right people. But as the violence escalated, Faulkner became more and more insistent. On July 9th he telephoned Heath [British Tory PM]. "I must be able to intern now", he demanded. Accordingly, with some reluctance, a 'dry run' was agreed upon. At dawn on 23rd July 1,800 troops and RUC raided republican houses throughout the province, searching for documents. They got enough to encourage them. The decision to intern was only a matter of time then, despite army objections. *(p85)*

Chapter 8 of McGuffin's work deals with those actually interned:

> The initial internment sweep on 9th August 1971 was, militarily, a

> complete failure. The IRA had known of it for some time and as a result
> virtually every senior IRA man was billeted away from home. Of the 342
> men arrested (the British army tried for 450), 116 men were released
> within 48 hours. 226 men were detained: 86 from Belfast, 60 from
> Co. Derry, 20 from the Newry area, 20 from Armagh and 40 from
> Fermanagh and Tyrone. Initially, 124 men were held in C wing of
> Crumlin (the number was to rise to 160 within five weeks) while the
> remainder were held on the Maidstone (prison ship).
>
> Within days Unionist ministers were claiming a fantastic success – a
> lie which subsequently caused them great embarrassment. Faulkner
> claimed 80 IRA officers arrested; the British GOC claimed 70% of
> terrorists on the wanted list. The claims could not have been further from
> the truth. Of the 160 men in Crumlin, no more than 80 had anything to
> do with the IRA, and of these only four were senior officers (none of
> them the top men). The rest of the internees were political opponents of
> the Unionists – like the PD and NICRA members, old retired IRA ex-
> internees, militant trade unionists, public speakers, and, in some cases,
> people held on mistaken identity   (p87)

Faulkner was determined to silence any street opposition to his draconian measures, as he envisaged the sweeps would continue for at least six months. During that time 2,357 were arrested under the Special Powers Act, 598 interned, 159 detained, and 1,600 completely innocent men (even by the government's standards) released after 'interrogation' – nearly 67 per cent.

He thought he could simply declare a ban on all public demonstrations for a period of twelve months, in the likely hope that 'moderate' figures and churchmen within the nationalist community would help him dampen mass agitation, thereby assisting his repressive strategy. The introduction of internment yet again had a unifying effect on the nationalist community. Serious disorders marked the occasion, with his ban on marches being defied in broad daylight. During the hours of darkness the Catholic ghettos had their night-shifts of protesters. Women clattered bin-lids at the approach of British and police raiding parties. Youths repainted slogans or murals obliterated by the Crown forces, removed street signs, door numbers and selected street lighting to bother, confuse and disorientate them as well.

The first weeks after August 9th showed that, rather than end political violence, internment actually exacerbated the situation, with 35 people having been killed as a result. A widespread rent and rates strike followed, which had the support of tens of thousands of households. Posters to this effect appeared in windows all over the occupied area – as well as the more contemptuously militant slogan, 'Rent Spent!' By October the effectiveness of the strike became apparent. In Newry there was 95 per cent non-payment, with its Urban Council losing £150,000 in ten weeks. In Lurgan the decline was £10,000 per week. In Derry, the Creggan estate alone had 15,000 refuseniks with a 98 per cent success rate for the strike, whereas the Bogside and Brandywell had 90 per cent; Coalisland (Tyrone) 95 per cent; Andersontown (Belfast) had 80 per cent refusing to pay. Gas and electricity bills, car tax, ground rent, TV licences and fines to courts were quickly added to the non-payment campaign. Soon even the dogs in the street would bark at the Brits without a licence. Local government virtually ground to a halt.

The Northern Ireland Civil Rights Association, however, refused to take to the streets. Their logic was simple – you couldn't march because it was illegal and they might put you in jail if you did! Other bodies like the Civil Resistance Committees, and the Northern Resistance Movement began to grow out of the resentment and frustration which was keenly felt at the time. Finally, with the full support of the internees in Long Kesh, a group of trade unionists in Tyrone (in co-operation with Belfast and Armagh militants including the PD) called a march for Christmas Day. It assembled at Beechmont in Belfast, and despite atrocious weather conditions moved off in heavy snow for the new concentration camp some ten miles away. An estimated 4,000 people participated. The British army's attempts to stop the demonstration failed. The march was a great morale-booster. The British laws had been flouted and the floodgates were opened. NICRA shamefacedly had to call their own march – straight up the Falls to the heart of the ghetto. But the marching season was on. Marches at Magilligan internment camp, more protests at the Long Kesh camp and finally the march in Derry which was to be remembered as 'Bloody Sunday'.

Within days of the internment swoops, stories began to filter out of the concentration camps, Crumlin jail and the prison ship Maidstone indicating that severe torture had been used against numerous internees. As time progressed the extent of such tortures was fully realised and confirmed. By mid-October the British newspapers, particularly the *Sunday Times*, had taken up the story and reported on "third degree tortures and interrogation". The majority of the British media ignored the allegations, and like an ostrich when being pursued, buried their head in the sand. The *Sunday Times* had, however, only published something which had been known in Ireland for two months previously. In fact the Association for Legal Justice (ALJ) had collected and distributed statements to the press as far back as August 20th. In the first week of September the British press was circulated with a ten page dossier compiled by the London Anti-Internment League, based largely on ALJ research, but the British public only got a glimpse of what was happening some five weeks later. This was due to a number of factors, but in the main journalists adopted a policy of self-censorship. What they did not wish to believe, they did not write about. The most outstanding journalists of this period were: the staff of *Private Eye*; Jonathan Dimbleby of the BBC's 'World at One' programme who had the courage to declare, "it's got to the stage where we're being repressed"; Roy Bull of the *Scotsman* who framed a declaration for the Free Communications Group which read: "We deplore the intensification of censorship on TV, radio and the press coverage of events in N. Ireland and pledge ourselves to oppose it"; and Keith Kyle who attacked those who claimed censorship was 'in the national interest' by retorting, "there is no higher national interest than avoiding self-deception on Northern Ireland."

This was the background to the protests which occurred between August 9th 1971 and January 30th 1972. The reasons for the marches etc, were not merely to protest against internment, but to expose to the world the terrible and foul tortures endured by helpless detainees. The attitude of the British media was a factor that made many thinking people within the expanding protest movements realise that the facts associated with internment could only be conveyed to the world via mass street agitation. If they obeyed Faulkner's ban, the world might never know, and the tortures might increase. By physically and intellectually opposing the ban and the Special Powers Act it was hoped to not only smash internment but to make censorship itself prove worthless. By so doing the world beyond our shores slowly began to realise what was happening in this antiquated, British-controlled statelet.

The dreaded knock on the door at dawn, or the splintering of locks from door frames and the physical removal of fellow citizens from their homes amid great family distress, were images that united entire communities. Those who lived through those days hardly need to refresh their memories as each anniversary of internment and Bloody Sunday falls due. The torture of the prisoners, besides the circumstances of their immediate arrest, will forever remain facts of history, yet the detail is important to recall and record. It was such detail that drove the people onto the streets so that others too might be made aware of the situation. Several were to forfeit their lives for so doing.

The following is one case of torture, which is by no means exceptional, as others taken in the first round-ups suffered similarly. The case appeared as a report in a small circulation publication, *Socialist Voice*, written jointly by Londoners Sean Hallahan and Chris Dolan. Under the heading, 'Strasbourg Horror Tale of Army Terror in Ulster', it begins:

> The case of the Hooded Men of Strasbourg is not some rediscovered manuscript by Arthur Conan Doyle or the title of a new film by Hammer. There is plenty of horror in the story but it is all too real, owing nothing to the special effects department of any film company. The 'Hooded Men' are a group of Irishmen who were lifted by the British army on August 9th 1971 and subjected to systematic torture by the forces of 'law and order'. Their cases are currently being discussed at the European Court in Strasbourg and it is the British government that is on trial. This is the story of what happened to one of those men, Michael Montgomery of Derry, who was active in the civil rights movement and later became the first republican councillor for Derry City since the 1920s. He is a member of the Irish Republican Socialist Party. On August 9th 1971, Michael was dragged from his bed by British soldiers and thrown into a Saracen armoured car while his wife and children were left crying helplessly. Mick, as he likes to be called, was driven to a nearby army barracks where he recognised members of the RUC Special Branch. He was taken from there by furniture van to Magilligan camp (later to be an internment centre) and left with others who had been lifted to stand two hours in the rain. His requests to see a solicitor were refused. He was questioned twice in six hours and refused to answer questions other than his name and address.
>
> A hood was then placed over his head by members of the RUC and he was put into a helicopter which rose from the ground several feet. Mick was then thrown out! He was returned to the 'copter and flown to another place and told to lean against the wall on his fingertips. After examination by a British army doctor he was placed in a room where there was a continual noise like that of escaping steam. He was told to lie on the ground and his legs were forced apart until it felt "like my back passage was splitting". He passed out. He awoke and his testicles were massaged with the sole of a rubber boot until they were swollen. Mick

*was again forced to stand against a wall resting on his fingertips.
Throughout this ordeal he was being repeatedly beaten, often to the
point of unconsciousness. At some time a tube was inserted in his anus
and he passed out again. His requests for water were granted – but
instead of being allowed to drink it the security forces threw it over the
hood – making breathing even more difficult. Another factor that made
breathing difficult was that while being beaten Mick had vomited and the
vomit accumulated inside the hood.*

*During much of this period no words were spoken by the torturers
and Mick had the idea that this was to confuse him, so that he could not
say whether he was being tortured by the RUC or the British army. By
this time he had lost all track of time. At certain periods he was taken for
interrogation and asked about the IRA and left-wing groups. At one point
he heard the click of a revolver and was told that his wife and children
had been shot. During some of the time Mick was hallucinating. At
intervals he was allowed to sleep and was 'fed' when bread was forced
down his throat, from under the hood. He was told he was in the
Channel Isles, and then one day, that he was going home. He was taken
by helicopter (after being shaved and deodorised) not home, but to
Belfast's Crumlin Road jail. In jail he was examined by a doctor and Mick
asked him what day it was. The doctor replied that it was a Tuesday and
Mick expressed disbelief. August 9th was a Monday and Mick knew he
had been held for more than 24 hours. He had – it was the Tuesday of
the following week and the ordeal had taken over eight days!*

John McGuffin's hard-hitting work spares no punches. He wrote:

*Torture and brutality are emotive words. They are words used frequently
by propagandists. Nonetheless, in the Northern Ireland context, in the
year 1971-1972, they are more honest words than the emasculated
semantics of Sir Edmund Compton or the bland lies of Brian Faulkner
and General Tuzo. For the simple fact is that brutality by the British army
became so usual as to be commonplace, while torture was systematically
– and generally inefficiently – carried out by both army intelligence and
the RUC Special Branch on an increasing scale.*   *(p116)*

Torture took place at several locations, but the two main centres
were the compounds of Palace Barracks, Holywood, and at Girdwood
Park camp which adjoins Crumlin Jail, Belfast. A distance of a mere five
miles separated the two. Palace Barracks was the HQ of the 1st Parachute
Regiment, which had billeted there members of the undercover 22nd
Special Air Service Regiment. The torture compound consisted of four

huts surrounded by a corrugated iron perimeter wall. It was deliberately located well to the rear of the camp and could not be seen from the road.

Girdwood contained many armed military policemen, the majority of whom took turns at beating, threatening and sadistically maltreating these uncharged civilians, supposedly in their care. Barefoot detainees were forced to run over broken glass, and at this location the 'helicopter treatment' proved a popular terror tactic. Prisoners were to relate that Ballykinlar and Magilligan had even worse treatment on offer. These tortures went on for months, and covered four distinct phases. As late as November 1971 authenticated reports of electric shock treatment were coming out of the interrogation centres and were common knowledge. Between October and 24th January over 20 men had been subjected to this form of interrogation. This was eventually confirmed several weeks later, again, in London by the *Sunday Times*, on March 5th 1972, while the rest of the British press were still engaged in self-censorship.

It was the factual reports, however, released in Ireland, often within days of the actual tortures, that drove the nationalist population onto the streets to cry for justice. Each distinct phase was being carefully recorded for local and international agencies by the non-political ALJ and figures such as Fr. Denis Faul and Fr. Raymond Murray, both Catholic priests well-known as hostile to the republican struggle. By late November 'the drugs phase' had been introduced, with two types clearly identified which were being used on selected detainees. This was confirmed by urine samples medically tested at the request of solicitors on the release of several detainees.

They were not content with torturing captive Irishmen and women. Few of those on the outside, who were about to march in Derry, would have believed what was being planned for them behind the scenes, along the corridors of power. Both the Unionist and Tory leadership were mutually engaged in moves which would in effect amount to imposing the death penalty, again without the trappings of a trial, upon all those who would dare to march against state repression through their own ghetto streets. On January 28th a special meeting of the British Cabinet's Defence and Overseas Committee attracted the top brass of the British ruling-elite, including William Whitelaw, the new Northern overseer, as well as other Cabinet ministers. Such an august gathering of British establishment figures were hardly discussing a mere snatch squad arrest operation, and it would seem clear that two major factors were on their minds.

The first was how best to maintain Brian Faulkner in power and preserve the puppet parliament at Stormont; and the second was how best to bring to an end the Free Derry no-go area which had been securely barricaded and refused to accept the British occupation and their uniformed Orange allies since 1969. The latter reality was a continuing affront to establishment ideas of what passes for 'good order'.

No doubt listening to the advocates of General Frank Kitson (who developed the British army strategy of psychological warfare and counter-subversion), on the second issue it was hoped that they could separate the fish (the IRA) from the water in which they swam (the people). The aim was to force the guerrilla forces out into the open by making them defend the people and the popularly declared liberated zone, Free Derry. Banning the demonstration could provide a smoke-screen or excuse for military intervention, for as far as high ranking strategists like Kitson were concerned, to use his own phrase, "the law is just another weapon in the government's arsenal... little more than a propaganda cover for the disposal of unwanted members of the public." Kitson had served in Kenya, Malaya and Cyprus before commanding the 39th Infantry Brigade in the Six Counties, 1970-72, and his work, 'Low-Intensity Operations', clearly reveals just how far the 'democratic' state can be manipulated by its own elites. Some comments made at the time, particularly those of none other than Lord Balneil, give a great deal of credit to this hypothesis. It may take many years, (the '30-year rule' for disclosures has been imposed) for the full story to see the light of day, but one thing is sure, British strategy must surely have misfired yet again. Not only did Faulkner fall, certainly as a result of internment, its aftermath, and the events of Bloody Sunday, but his puppet parliament also fell by the end of March 1972. This took almost everyone by surprise, and had seemed impossible only a few short months before.

Whitehall watchers include many from the North and there were signs of 'something big' on the cards. The IRA leadership must be numbered among the observers and may well have smelt a rat with the drafting in of the 1st Paras, the so-called 'crack regiment', to handle a routinely planned peaceful civil rights demonstration. The republican forces would never have been so foolish as to oblige the British Cabinet and its generals by coming out openly on the streets in the fashion the latter would obviously have desired. Guerrilla armies rarely take on a conventional-style offensive. Another fact worthy of mention: civil rights demonstrators never allowed any display of militarism at marches, would be physically hostile to such displays and genuinely embraced the ideology of non-violent public protest. Amid great danger since Duke Street, and even immediately after Bloody Sunday, people clung to the need to remain on the streets with their bodies and voices as their only weapons of struggle. This is a heroism based on the justice of one's case, that has no need for militarist trappings as inner strength expressed by whole communities has often overcome entire armies.

In retrospect, it is easy to pin-point some ominous signs which appeared prior to January 30th. A meeting organised by the Rev. Ian Kyle Paisley was suddenly called off, and this was coupled with a warning to 'all loyalists' to steer clear of the city centre. On Tuesday January 25th, the *Guardian*, in a front-page headline, gave a clue as to the type of troops and their likely conduct in Derry on the following Sunday afternoon. The report bore the heading, 'CO's want Paras restrained', and written by Simon Hoggart, a journalist of some note then in Belfast, informed readers that:

> At least two British army units in Belfast made informal requests to brigade headquarters for the Parachute Regiment to be kept out of their areas. Senior officers in these units regard the paratroop's tactics as too rough and on occasion, brutal. One officer in a troubled area, whose commanding officer made such a request, said: "The Paras undid in 10 minutes community relations which it has taken us four weeks to build up". News of the requests, which to say the least are extraordinary within the British army, came after the Parachute Regiment had completed its own investigations of the weekend's events at Magilligan internment camp, when reporters saw paratroopers club demonstrators and fire rubber bullets at point blank range. Since the requests were made paratroopers have not been used in these sensitive areas of Belfast which are thought to be beginning to calm down. This is because the army believes the absolute minimum of force must be used to prevent the local community from becoming more disaffected with the army. Undoubtedly the regiment is the one most hated by Catholics in troubled areas, where it has, among local people at least, a reputation for brutality. A Captain in one regiment whose CO has not made a request said: "They are frankly disliked by many officers here, who regard some of their men as little more than thugs in uniform. I have seen them arrive on the scene, thump up a few people who might be doing nothing more than shouting and jeering, they seem to think that they can get away with whatever they like..."

So spoke a Brit Captain, but his last sentence was certainly proven correct, insofar as none of the Bloody Sunday murderers ever faced trial and their Commanding Officer, Col Derek Wilford was decorated by the English Queen for "outstanding service to the Crown" less than twelve months after the massacre.

It was a rare day of sunshine as the crowd, numbering several thousands, including children, gathered in Creggan. A jovial 'fair day' atmosphere prevailed as the marchers moved in disarray descending the hill towards the Bogside and William Street, down which they hoped to walk into the nearby Guildhall Square. The march had started off from the Bishop's Field, a determined but still good humoured demonstration that was simply out to show its deep-rooted abhorrence of internment without charge or trial and the torture and brutality that had been associated with this policy since August 9th. They had marched to and assembled in Guildhall Square before, so why should anything be different this time? The Stormont government's ban on parades was shattered as the march moved over a three-mile route. The plan included walking down the steep horse-shoe at Southway, which led onto the Lone Moor Road, winding down Stanley's Walk along the old gas yard wall leading into Lecky Road, followed by the climb up Westland Street, along Laburnum Terrace, Marlborough Terrace and down to the Creggan Street roundabout which was the start of William Street and the last few hundreds yards. Traditionally people gathered at local street corners waiting for the march to come along, and before too long it was growing steadily until the slow-moving human throng was being estimated by the press at around 27,000. At the bottom of each hill people looked up at the large numbers in front of them, and on the crest of each hill they looked back to comment on the larger numbers behind. In front as always were the Civil Rights Association banners, this time flanked by the younger participants who carried placards bearing the names of the Derry internees, some of whom were their brothers, fathers, uncles or cousins.

As the massive parade reached the William Street and Rossville Street junction, the lorry carrying senior civil rights officials turned right into Rossville Street, but a small section of the crowd continued on down William Street until it came up against an army barrier of vehicles at the old City Cinema site. Some stayed to throw stones, bottles and pieces of wood at the well protected troops, but the confrontation never reached serious proportions and the protesters had no chance of breaking through to Guildhall Square. The throwing of missiles was mere symbolism for the militant youth, and such in fact was a minor incident compared with some of the earlier confrontations that occurred in the same vicinity, when no civil rights stewards were on hand to insist on non-violent protest. A female steward was led away bleeding from a head wound after being hit by a stone. An army water cannon then moved up to their barrier and sprayed the demonstrators with purple dye. The crowd scattered into Chamberlain Street and other entrances to the Bogside. The majority of the marchers had by now moved to Free Derry Corner. The Paras, supported by Saracens, moved into Rossville Street on what, according to an army spokesman later, was an arrest and search operation. The Saracens roared into the car park at the high flats as the stragglers in the crowd fled in various directions.

Meanwhile at Free Derry Corner attempts were being made to get the anti-internment meeting, earlier scheduled for Guildhall Square, under way. The meeting was just about to commence, with Lord Fenner Brockway, MP, and other speakers on the platform, when the whine of bullets was heard to the disbelief of all present. Over the Bogside the CS gas was drifting, amid the thud of rubber bullets, salvoes of them. This sound was broken by the sharper cracks of live rounds, whining viciously on their death-dealing way. The immediate reaction of the people at the meeting was to dive full-length on the ground, as a number of rounds hit the wall of Free Derry Corner, directly above the speakers' heads. For minutes the firing continued amid screaming and great confusion. Then came a blessed lull. People got to their feet and made for St Columb's Wells. But again, within a few seconds, people hit the ground as more bullets whined about. Eventually many, bent double, got into the comparative safety of 'The Wells'.

Further down the street, at the Rossville Flats, Glenfada Park, and at the rubble barricade opposite the entrance to the high flats and other open spaces, people were being hit by British sniper fire using high velocity weapons. To the crowd at Free Derry Corner, the stark, stunning realisation of what had really happened began to sink in. Four men came into The Wells carrying another man, wounded in the back as he ran for cover, his face grey and grimacing with the pain. He was put into a car and rushed immediately to the hospital. Then more wounded were carried in. Immediately cars appeared to take them away for medical attention. Five wounded were taken away in the space of a few minutes. Other cars came racing along into The Wells, none of them stopping, as they made their way to Altnagelvin Hospital, near the city outskirts on the east bank of the River Foyle. Some were already dead before they reached the hospital complex.

But the full horror of the day's tragic events was happening in the neighbourhood of the high flats. As the Saracens and paratroopers stormed into the area – shooting as they came, according to eye-witnesses – the crowd scattered in all directions. It was then, as people sought shelter, that most of the killings took place. Priests and members of the Knights of Malta (first aid organisation) moved about the area attending the wounded or administering the Last Rites while British bullets whistled around them. Sporadic firing continued to echo around the courtyards as the injured were lifted into cars and ambulances. In Rossville Street several bodies lay covered with blankets as Fr. Edward Daly (now Bishop of Derry) waving his white handkerchief in the air, led stretcher-bearers across the street to the waiting ar bulances.

Within hours of the butchery, a silent, shuttered Derry mourned its dead. Factories, shops, stores, banks and offices all closed down, as happened in other parts of Ireland, as a nation participated in mute but eloquent protest. Thinner than usual traffic moved down streets peopled only at occasional corners by heavily-armed, jumpily alert, British soldiers. It seemed that almost the whole population had voluntarily vacated the open air to grieve in private yet community-wide sorrow. But underneath the calm exterior, resentment, anger, revulsion and shock blended in a population still stunned by the enormity of the city's disaster. Beneath and behind it all there was a determination that the British army of occupation had long outstayed its 'welcome' and that the nationalist majority were determined to work for the speedy removal of the troops, initially from the streets of Derry's west bank, and eventually from the whole of Ireland.

On the day of the funerals, Wednesday February 2nd, nationalist Ireland was united in grief. St Mary's Church in the Creggan estate was the centre of world attention for the poignant hour while Derry buried its dead. Church and state, people, priests and politicians joined in a unique ceremony which expressed the emotion of a sorrowing nation. From North and South, from East and West they came, the mourning tens of thousands, to honour the dead, to comfort the bereaved, to pledge by their living presence a humane response to another horrible tragedy in Ireland's long history of imperialist conquest. There were few dry eyes among the congregation. Outside the thronging thousands ignored the bitter cold, and in the driving rain it seemed that even the skies wept, and the heavens could not hold back their tears.

Two days after the slaughter of thirteen innocent civil rights demonstrators, eight of the wounded, all Derry people, spoke to the world from their hospital beds. All eight unanimously denied a British army claim that two of the men in the hospital had admitted that they were carrying arms on that Sunday. Alexander Nash, aged 52, of 38 Dunree Gardens who saw his son William shot dead, told how he himself got his arm and body wounds. He said:

> I saw the troops throw three bodies into a Saracen like pigs. I went to where my son was lying on the ground and raised my arms. I was shot as I moved across.

Joseph Friel, aged 20 of Donagh Place said he was in Meenan Park:

> While lying there I was told that several people were dead and I cried. I thought at first I was hit by a plastic bullet. I think my life was saved by a bullet deflecting from a zip fastener. After I was shot I was taken into a house. I never lost consciousness, but I thought I was going to die. The army shot indiscriminately. I suppose I will lose my job for talking to the press because I work for the Queen in the Tax Office, but after what happened in Derry I don't care. I want the truth to be known.

Mr Friel was shot in the chest.

Michael Bridge, aged 25, of 10 Termore Gardens, said he was at the back of Rossville Street flats. When he heard shots, he and other men rushed out to see what was happening. Troops were shouting. A priest was kneeling over a man who had been shot:

> As I went forward troops fired several shots. I think they were trying to shoot the priest, who I think was Fr. Daly.

Patrick Campbell, aged 53, of 4 Carrickreagh Gardens, who was shot in the back, said he was shot while running away in Rossville Street. The soldiers were firing indiscriminately. Michael Bradley, aged 22, of Rinmore Drive, who was shot also in the back said:

> It was just like an ambush. Troops were firing all around.

Mr Bradley said that he did not see anyone firing at the troops. He admitted that they threw stones at the troops in William Street after the troops opened fire.

Patrick O'Donnell, aged 40, a foreman asphalt spreader, of 10 Rathowen Drive, said he was shot when he went to the aid of a woman he thought a soldier was aiming at. He tried to pull the woman down, and fell himself, in the hope that he would be safe but he felt a pain and knew he had been shot in the shoulder. Mr O'Donnell said that he was subsequently manhandled by troops and he showed two cuts on his head received when he was batoned. The troops took him into William Street from Rossville Street, but there an officer said: "Leave the man alone. He is hurt." The same officer told the soldiers to let him go and after being taken home in a taxi he was subsequently taken to Altnagelvin Hospital by his own doctor. He saw nobody shooting at soldiers.

Patrick McDaid, aged 24, of Dunaff Gardens, said he heard everyone shouting "the soldiers are coming!" He saw a couple of young fellows coming round the corner carrying a woman. Then he heard people shout:

"They are shooting everyone!" I ran too, and at the corner of Rossville Street I bent down to dive low. As I did something hit me in the shoulder and back. If I hadn't bent down, I would have been hit in the head.

The names of others wounded on Bloody Sunday were released by Altnagelvin Hospital on January 31st. These included: Joseph Mahon, aged 16, Rathkeale Way, whose condition was stated to be ill; Alana Burke, aged 19, of Bishop Street, satisfactory; Margaret Deery, aged 37, Swilly Gardens, satisfactory.

A list of the wounded appeared in a shop window in the Bogside. Other names included on this list were: Mr M. Quinn, Marlborough Street; Johnny Johnson (who later died of his wounds), Marlborough Street; Mr Campbell, Carrickreagh Gardens; Mr O'Donnell, Rathowen Park; Mr McKeown, Lone Moore Road; Mr D. Donaghy, Rinmore Drive; Mr McDaid, address not known; and Ann Richmond of Swilly Gardens.

Rev. Fr. Edward Daly, Catholic Curate St Eugene's Cathedral, told journalists:

The British army should hang its head in shame after today's disgusting violence. They shot indiscriminately and everywhere around them without any provocation. It appeared as though the paratroopers were under orders to move in and shoot away at anyone. A 16 year-old boy was shot beside me, and others were badly injured by the firing. I crawled to him and gave him the Last Rites for there was no hope of saving his life. The quicker the British army get out of the Six Counties after today's violence, the better for everyone concerned. It is the only way to achieve peace. There has been a terrible amount of blood, and no public relations job by the British army will cover this up. I intend to protest to the highest people in the strongest way possible.

Eddie McAteer, president of the Irish Nationalist Party, and Official

Opposition leader in the Stormont Parliament said:

> I saw the first two people shot, a teenager and an elderly man, both falling in William Street. It was a simple massacre. There were no petrol bombs, no guns, no snipers, no justification whatsoever for this well-organised slaughter. Derry's Bloody Sunday will be remembered as the British army's greatest day of shame.

Mr Michael Canavan, chairperson, of the Citizens' Central Committee, and former honorary treasurer of the Derry Citizens' Action Committee, commented:

> It was a massacre. The troops opened fire as Miss Devlin picked up the microphone to address the huge crowd at Free Derry Corner.

Bernadette Devlin, former Westminster MP said:

> Let nobody say the British army fired in retaliation.

Mr Finbarr O'Kane, civil rights leader stated:

> Lord Brockway was on the platform waiting to address the crowd, when a bullet hit a wall nearby. People didn't realise what it was at first, but more shooting started and everybody hit the ground. The shooting seemed to stop after a bit and everyone got up on all fours and started to crawl away. But it started again. I've never seen anything like it. Everybody was trying to crawl away, hitting walls and stumbling.

Signor Fulvio Grimaldi, a visiting Italian journalist reported:

> There hadn't been one shot fired at them. There hadn't been one petrol bomb thrown at them. There hadn't been one nail bomb thrown at them. They just jumped out, and with unbelievable murderous fury, shot into the fleeing crowd. I have travelled in many countries. I have seen many civil wars and revolutions and wars. I have never seen such a cold-blooded murder, organised disciplined murder, planned murder. I saw a young fellow who had been wounded, crouching against the wall. He was shouting, "Don't shoot, don't shoot!" A paratrooper approached him and shot him from about one yard. I saw a young boy of 15 protecting his girlfriend against a wall and then proceeding to try and rescue her by going out with a handkerchief and with the other hand on his hat. A paratrooper approached, shot him from about one yard into the stomach, and shot the girl into the arm. I saw a priest approaching a fallen boy in the middle of the square, trying to help him, give him the Last Rites perhaps – I saw a paratrooper kneel down and take aim at him and shoot at him, and the priest just got away by laying flat on his belly. I saw a French colleague of mine, who shouting "Press, Press!" and raising high his arms, went into the middle to give help to a fallen person.

I saw the para again kneeling down and aiming at him, and it's only by a
fantastic acrobatic jump that he got away.

The Italian journalist, almost lost for words, concluded:

I myself got shot at five times. I was certain at one stage of being hit as I
was taking photos through a window. I approached the window to get
some pictures of what was happening, and five shots immediately went
through the glass. I don't know how they missed. The mood of the people
while this was going on? It was panic, it was sheer despair, it was
frustration. I saw people crying, old men crying, young boys who had lost
their friends only a short while before crying and not understanding.
There was astonishment. There was bewilderment, there was rage and
frustration. It was unbelievable…

The local Official Republican newspaper, the *Starry Plough,* in its
editorial commented:

Bloody Sunday was carried out with one objective. The British army
decided coldly and deliberately to shoot the risen people off the
streets. We were shot with our backs turned, in some cases, with our
hands in the air as we went to rescue the wounded. We were killed
on the barricades, in the courtyards and a few died God knows
where. The vultures picked them up first. But the siege goes on. The
808 acres of Bogside, Brandywell and the Creggan remain free. Forty
of the forty-two entrances to Free Derry remain barricaded. Sunday,
Bloody Sunday, was a fine day and a foul day. It was a fine thing to
swing down Southway, thousands of us singing, to pick thousands
more of our comrades at the Brandywell. And then to swell through
the Bogside where it all began four years ago. Do you remember?…
We asked them to ban the Corporation, and they said no, and then
they banned it. We demanded houses and they said no, and then
they built them. We demanded that Craig should go, and they said
no, and then he went. We told the police to leave the Bogside and
they said no – running all the way back to barracks. And when Sam
Devenney died, paying the price of it all, we thought it more than we
could bear, but we did. Death was strange then, Death is no stranger
now, but the price is higher and no easier to bear. No one who died
was a stranger to us. What impossible things did we demand this
time? That our internees be freed? That we walk on our own streets,
that the Stormont cesspool be cleaned up – even the SDLP couldn't
bear the stink. For the least of these and the best of these, thirteen
men were murdered last week. Let it be said of them with pride,

they died on their feet and not on their knees. Let it not be said of
us, they died in vain.
STAY FREE, BROTHERS AND SISTERS,
THERE'LL BE ANOTHER DAY!

The original British army version of events – as given in an official statement in the Commons by the Minister of Defence – was viewed by many as a tangle of lies. They claimed they opened fire after coming under attack from nail bombers and "a fusillade of fire of 50-80 shots from the area of Rossville and Glenfada flats". The international media were anxious to find proof in support of such accusations. No independent witness from among the scores of journalists and other observers – including pro-Unionist columnists – accepted the claim that the IRA was actively engaged on the day, and rejected the British establishment's contentions. When all was said and done, the British forces could not produce either the bullet or the bomb fragments.

The British forces claimed that "in all cases soldiers fired aimed shots at men identified as gunmen and bombers." Forensic tests on those killed failed to establish that any of the thirteen were in contact with any weapons: no weapons were found on those killed or rounded-up; no charges were brought against those wounded.

The British army further said that some of those shot were on their wanted list: this was later easily disproved. They said they shot three snipers in the flats, but all the casualties were at ground level. The British army stories had virtually no supporters outside the military establishment itself. Britain, however, had to save its face as best it could, especially in the United States, where there was then a considerable Irish lobby, which might be inclined to swing towards those engaged in the physical force and resistance movements in 'the old country'. So, after Bloody Sunday, the British government set up a 'Tribunal of Inquiry' – misnamed for it consisted of only one man, former army officer Lord Widgery. Subsequently, nationalist writers and spokespersons would refer to this inquiry, supposedly appointed to establish the truth, as 'the cover-up'. Even prominent British and other foreign journalists were to use the same descriptive term in their reportage.

Although Widgery's report was a whitewash and full of contradictions, it nevertheless contained some criticisms of the British army. But the British public was never to hear these criticisms because of the way the Ministry of Defence handled the press and the way the press, almost without exception, played along.

Simon Winchester, a British journalist with the *Guardian* who was present on Bloody Sunday and had personally narrowly escaped the Paras' bullets, writes in his book 'In Holy Terror':

Widgery's conclusions were at astonishing variance with his own report; and the manner of the 'leaking' of the document itself was an appalling travesty of honesty, for which both the British press and the British government should feel ashamed.

In spite of his own evidence which showed among other things that large numbers of unaccounted-for rounds and 'unjustifiably dangerous' shots had been fired by the Paras, Widgery concluded by exonerating the army:

There is no clear reason to suppose that the soldiers would have opened fire if they had not been fired upon first. Soldiers who identified armed gunmen fired upon them in accordance with the standing orders in the Yellow Card. There was no general breakdown in discipline.

Winchester describes what happened when the report was completed:

The report itself was to be issued on the afternoon of Wednesday April 19th. In fact, the astute press officers of the Ministry of Defence telephoned the Defence Correspondents of the national newspapers the night before to 'leak' in highly selective terms the Lord's conclusions to be published the next day. No mention was made in the 'leak' of any "underestimate of the dangers" (involved in launching the Paras' operation), of any army gunfire that "bordered on the reckless" as Widgery remarked in Conclusion Number 8. Those who read their front pages on Wednesday morning would have had to have been very short-sighted indeed to have missed the results of the PR work. 'Widgery Clears Army!' they shrieked in near unison; and a relieved British public read no more. Bloody Sunday, thanks to the propaganda merchants and a half dozen lazy hacks, was now a closed book, with the Irish fully to blame.

THE BLOODY SUNDAY DEAD

MICHAEL KELLY (17) an apprentice electrician employed at Maydown. He resided at 9 Dunmore Gardens, Creggan.

JOHN YOUNG (17) who resided at Westway, Creggan. He was a salesman and was the youngest of a family of six.

PATRICK DOHERTY (30) of Hamilton Street, Brandywell, who for six years before he died was engaged in construction work at Du Pont, Maydown.

HUGH GILMOUR (17) who resided at Garvan Place, in the Bogside.

WILLIAM NASH (19) who resided at Dunree Gardens, Creggan. A dock worker and a member of a famous boxing family.

JAMES JOSEPH WRAY (23) who resided at Drumcliff Avenue, in the Bogside, had worked at Lec Refrigerators.

WILLIAM McKINNEY (27) who resided at 62 Westway, Creggan. He was the eldest of a family of ten. A printer employed by the *Derry Journal* newspaper.

KEVIN McELHINNEY (17) a grocery assistant of 44 Philip St. He was one of a family of five.

BERNARD McGUIGAN (41) who resided at 20 Iniscarn Crescent, Creggan. An ex-foreman in the BSR, he was the father of six.

GERALD McKINNEY resided at Knockdarra House, Waterside, was the father of eight children, the youngest a baby boy born on February 7th 1972.

GERALD DONAGHY (17) resided at Meenan Square, in the Bogside. He was the youngest to die that day.

MICHAEL McDAID (21) a barman who resided at Tyrconnell Street in the Bogside.

JACK DUDDY (17) who resided at Central Drive in the Creggan Estate. He was a weaver in Thomas French's factory at Springtown Industrial estate. He was one of a family of fifteen.

JOHN JOHNSON who resided at Marlborough Street, who died on June 16th 1972. He was the first man to be shot on Bloody Sunday, near the centre of William Street.

APPENDIX I

Summary of the Special Powers Act

PREAMBLE

In April 1963, J. Vorster, at that time Minister of Justice in a racist police state, whilst introducing a new Coercion Bill in the South African parliament, could say that he "would be willing to exchange all the legislation of that sort for one clause of the Northern Ireland Special Powers Act". An enquiry carried out by the (British) National Council of Civil Liberties in 1936 commented that the Unionists had created "under the shadow of the British constitution a permanent machine of dictatorship". The NCCL compared Northern Ireland with the fascist dictatorships then current in Europe. This author would suggest that the Special Powers Act was retained in the Six Counties by ruling class bullies to intimidate a subject people, since it applied to no other region of the United Kingdom.

This Act, which had been continuously in operation since 1922, empowered the authorities to:

(1) Arrest without warrant.

(2) Imprison without charge or trial and deny recourse to Habeas Corpus or a court of law.

(3) Enter and search houses without warrant, and with force, at any hour of day or night.

(4) Declare a curfew and prohibit meetings, assemblies (including fairs and markets) and processions.

(5) Permit punishment by flogging ('cat-of-nine-tails').

(6) Deny any claim to a trial by jury.

(7) Arrest persons that police desired to examine as witnesses, forcibly detain them and compel them to answer questions, under penalties, even if answers might incriminate them. Such a person was guilty of an offence if he/she refused to be sworn or answer a question.

(8) Do any act involving interference with the rights of private property.

(9) Prevent access of relatives or legal advisers to a person imprisoned without trial.

(10) Prohibit the holding of an inquest after a prisoner's death.

(11) Arrest a person who 'by word of mouth' spreads false reports or makes false statements.

(12) Prohibit the circulation of any newspaper, e.g. the *United Irishman* etc.

(13) Prohibit the possession of any film, or gramophone record.

(14) Arrest a person who does anything "calculated to be prejudicial to the preservation of peace or maintenance of order in Northern Ireland and not specifically provided for in the regulations."

(15) The Act allows the Minister of Home Affairs to create new crimes by government decree, e.g. it became a crime to name a club a 'Republican Club'.

Flags and Emblems (Display) Act (Northern Ireland) 1954

The main provision of this Act was:

"Where any police officer, having regard to the time and place at which and the circumstances in which any emblem is being displayed, apprehends that the display of such emblem may occasion a breach of the peace, he may require the person displaying or responsible for the display of such emblem to discontinue such display or cause it to be discontinued; and any person who refuses or fails to comply with such a requirement shall be guilty of an offence against this Act."

Such a guilty person being liable:

(a) on summary conviction, to a fine not exceeding fifty pounds or to imprisonment for a time not exceeding six months;

(b) on conviction on indictment, to a fine not exceeding five hundred pounds or to imprisonment for a term not exceeding five years or in any case to both the fine and the imprisonment.

N.B. In addition to the Special Powers Act and the Flags and Emblems (Display) Act 1954, there was also the Public Order Act 1951, which dealt specifically with processions and public meetings.

Quotes from Unionist leaders 1922-1969

SIR JAMES CRAIG (later VISCOUNT CRAIGAVON), Prime Minister of Northern Ireland 1921-40.

"It is also from the ranks of the Loyal Orange Institution that our splendid RUC 'Specials' have come." ('Belfast Newsletter', 13th July 1922)

"I have always said I am an Orangeman first and a politician and Member of Parliament afterwards… all I boast is that we are a Protestant Parliament and Protestant State." (24th April 1934, Parliamentary Debates, NI Vol XVI, Cols 1091-95).

Dame Enid Lyons, widow of Joseph A. Lyons, Prime Minister of Australia 1932-39, recalls in her memoirs ('So We Take Comfort', London 1965, p235) a famous gaffe illustrative of Craigavon's religious feelings.

"It was Lord Craigavon, the fiercely anti-Catholic Prime Minister of Northern Ireland, who knowing nothing of Joe's personal background, had asked him at a banquet, 'Lyons, have you got many Catholics in Australia?' 'Oh, about one in five' Joe replied. 'Well watch 'em, Lyons, watch 'em,' Craigavon had urged. 'They breed like bloody rabbits'."

SIR BASIL BROOKE (later VISCOUNT BROOKEBOROUGH), Minister of Agriculture 1933-41; Minister of Commerce 1941-43; Prime Minister 1943-63.

"There were a great number of Protestants and Orangemen who employed Roman Catholics. He felt he could speak freely on this subject as he had not a Roman Catholic about his own place. He would appeal to Loyalists, therefore, wherever possible, to employ good Protestant lads and lassies." ('Fermanagh Times', 13th July 1933)

"He made certain remarks regarding the employment of Roman Catholics

which created a certain amount of controversy. He now wished to say he did not intend to withdraw a single word of what he then said." ('Fermanagh Times', 17th August 1933)

"Thinking out the whole question carefully, I recommended those people who are Loyalists not to employ Roman Catholics, ninety-nine per cent of whom are disloyal. I want you to remember one point in regard to the employment of people who are disloyal. There are often difficulties in the way, but usually there are plenty of good men and women available, and the employers don't bother to employ them. You are disenfranchising yourselves in that way. You people who are employers have the ball at your feet. If you don't act properly now, before we know where we are we shall find ourselves in the minority instead of the majority." ('Londonderry Sentinel', 20th March 1934)

SIR DAWSON BATES, Minister of Home Affairs 1921-43.

Mr G. C. Duggan, a Protestant who was a civil servant in Belfast (1921-39) and who returned after war service to become Comptroller and Auditor-General (1945-49), wrote as follows in the *Irish Times* (4th May 1967):

"When it is remembered that the first Minister, Sir Dawson Bates, held that post for 22 years and had such a prejudice against Catholics that he made it clear to his Permanent Secretary that he did not want his most juvenile clerk, or typist, if a Papist, assigned for duty to his Ministry, what could one expect when it came to filling posts in the Judiciary, Clerkships of the Crown and Peace and Crown Solicitors?"

EDWARD ARCHDALE (later SIR EDWARD ARCHDALE), Minister of Agriculture 1921-33.

"A man in Fintona asked him how it was that he had over 50 per cent Roman Catholics in his Ministry. He thought that was too funny. He had 109 of a staff, and so far as he knew there were four Roman Catholics. Three of these were civil servants, turned over to him whom he had to take when he began." ('Northern Whig', 2nd April 1925)

SIR JOSEPH DAVISON, Orange Grand Master of Belfast, Senator 1935; Deputy Leader of the Senate 1941; died 1948.

"When will the Protestant employers of Northern Ireland recognise their duty to their Protestant brothers and sisters and employ them to the exclusion of Roman Catholics... it is time Protestant employers of Northern Ireland realised that whenever a Roman Catholic is brought into their

employment it means one Protestant vote less. It is our duty to pass the word along from this great demonstration and I suggest the slogan should be 'Protestants employ Protestants'." ('Northern Whig', 28th August 1933)

BRIAN FAULKNER, MP, Minister of Home Affairs 1959-63; Minister of Commerce 1963-69; Minister of Development 1969; in 1972 became the last Prime Minister at Stormont.

"The Church of Rome, he warned, ran a world-wide organisation – the most efficient political undertaking in the world. It controlled newspapers, radio and television stations and a hundred and one other avenues of propaganda. It was able to give vigorous publicity to any cause it espouses... that it favours Irish Republicanism today as whole-heartedly as it has done for generations past is universally recognised." ('Northern Whig', 13th July 1954)

"There is no reason why Orangemen individually and collectively should not interest themselves in the economic welfare of the community. I mean by that statement we should be anxious to find employment for our brothers." ('County Down, Spectator,' 17th July 1954)

"Of one thing, I for my part, have no doubt – if it should ever happen that Orangemen disassociate themselves from the political life of Ulster, both Ulster and the Orange institution are doomed... I have said before and I repeat today – the Orange Order is the backbone of Ulster." ('Irish News', 13th July 1960)

ALEX HUNTER, MP.

Mr Alex Hunter, MP, said "he had been recently horrified to learn that a local authority within the combined Orange district had appointed a Roman Catholic to represent them on the County Antrim Education Committee." ('Northern Whig', 13th July 1956)

E.C. FERGUSON, MP (resigned from Parliament in October 1949 to become Crown Solicitor for Co. Fermanagh).

"The nationalist majority in the county (i.e. Fermanagh) notwithstanding a reduction of 336 in the year, stands at 3,684. We must ultimately reduce and liquidate that majority. This county, I think it can be safely said, is a Unionist county. The atmosphere is Unionist. The Boards and properties are nearly all controlled by Unionists. But there is still this millstone around our necks." ('Irish News', 13th April 1948)

THOMAS LYONS, MP.

Mr Lyons said "that in the Castlederg district they stood firmly for Orangeism, Protestantism and Unionism. They all mean the same thing. A man who was a Protestant and not a Unionist had a 'kink' in his make-up. Such a person was not normal." ('Belfast Newsletter', 14th July 1947)

ALDERMAN GEORGE ELLIOT.

"We are not going to build houses in the South ward and cut a rod to beat ourselves later on. We are going to see that the right people are put into these houses and we are not making any apology for it." (At Enniskillen on 7th November 1963). ('Impartial Reporter', 14th November 1963)

SENATOR J E N BARNHILL.

"Charity begins at home. If we are going to employ people we should give preference to Unionists. I am not saying that we should sack nationalist employees, but if we are going to employ new men we should give preference to Unionists." (At Londonderry on 9th January 1964)

CAPTAIN TERENCE O'NEILL, Prime Minister 1963-1969.

"Protestant girl required for housework. Apply to The Hon Mrs Terence O'Neill, Glebe House, Ahoghill, Co Antrim." (Advertisement in 'Belfast Telegraph', November, 1959. Quoted by 'Sunday Times', London, 2nd March 1969)

"It is frightfully hard to explain to Protestants that if you give Roman Catholics a good job and a good house, they will live like Protestants, because they will see neighbours with cars and television sets. They will refuse to have 18 children, but if a Roman Catholic is jobless, and lives in the most ghastly hovel, he will rear 18 children on National Assistance. If you treat Roman Catholics with due consideration and kindness, they will live like Protestants in spite of the authoritative nature of their church." ('Belfast Telegraph', 10th May 1969)

MAJOR JAMES CHICHESTER-CLARK, Prime Minister, 1969.

"Indeed, I am proud to be in the (Orange) Order and those criticising it know nothing about it." ('Irish Weekly', 31st May 1969)

APPENDIX 4

Summary of a written submission to Initiative '92 as it subsequently appeared in 'A Citizens' Inquiry – The Opsahl Report on Northern Ireland', published jointly with The Lilliput Press Ltd, Dublin, May 1993.

MR FIONNBARRA ÓDOCHARTAIGH, from Derry, sharply criticises the fair employment record of the Northern Ireland Civil Service and its influence, as he perceives it, on equality legislation. He suggests that a new agency, under the aegis of the Anglo-Irish inter-governmental conference, should oversee reforms within the NICS. Mr ÓDochartaigh says that many nationalists regarded the Fair Employment Agency as a 'paper tiger' and maintains that its successor, the Fair Employment Commission, which he says is 'still tightly controlled by the NICS', is not a marked improvement. He calls for 'serious changes' in the relationship between the two organisations.

Mr O'Dochartaigh says that, in spite of inter-governmental agencies, the Anglo-Irish Agreement and greater nationalist representation based on hard-won electoral reforms, the one unresolved item of the original civil rights (movement) is religious discrimination in jobs. "Catholics are still two and a half times more likely to be unemployed than other sections of the workforce. As a result, for countless thousands, and youth in particular, this glaring statistic alone creates a sense of social alienation, firmly rooted in associated poverty and acute feelings of personal and community unfulfilment."

He accuses the British government of simply 'tinkering with the problem' in setting a target for Catholics in policy-making jobs in the NICS. The current religious makeup of the NICS, Mr ÓDochartaigh reports, is: 63.2 per cent Protestant; 36.8 per cent Catholic; with senior posts 85.5 per cent Protestant and 14.5 per cent Catholic. He says that civil liberties groups have argued that if Britain was serious about tackling religious discrimination in the workplace, it need only 'turn the economic screw' by linking it to governmental tendering and contract policies.

"Provision for taking such affirmative action was actually built into fair employment legislation as recently as 1989, in response to the

MacBride principles campaign in America, but has never been used. Only the mildest means of enforcement have been implemented. In the period 1989-91, the only punitive action by the Fair Employment Commission was to fine fourteen companies, who failed to comply with the statutory regulations, an average of £100; hardly more than a slight slap on the wrist."

('The Economy and Society' II, Discrimination, p327-8)

Bibliography

Unpublished sources include personal diaries, speeches, letters, minute books, questionnaires, court summons and taped interviews. These are complemented by reference to various newspapers and radical or agitational publications, as well as internal political discussion documents preserved by the author and acknowledged, where necessary, throughout the text.

PUBLISHED SOURCES

One Derry before 'the Troubles'
1916 Proclamation
Government of Ireland Act 1920
Census of Ireland 1911, Vol 3, Ulster, Cd. 6051-1, HMSO, London 1912
Census of Population 1961, General Register Office, N of Ireland, HMSO, Belfast, 1964
The Plain Truth, 2nd edition, CSJ pamphlet, 15.6.1969
University of Strathclyde Survey, 1979
Lockwood Report & Wilson Plan, HMSO, 1965
Disturbances in Northern Ireland, Report of the Commission appointed by the Governor of N. Ireland (Cameron Report), HMSO, Belfast, 1969
DUAC & DHAC internal research documents & questionnaires, 1965-70
Eye Witness in Northern Ireland, pamphlet by Aiden Corrigan, 1969

Two The Harvey Street eviction
Newsletters: *Spearhead* (YRA); *Reality* (DHAC)
Social and Economic Programme of the Republican Movement (1964-)
The United Irishman; The Derry Journal; Belfast Telegraph;
The Irish News

Three The homeless revolt
The Irish Militant (IWG)
Derry, Countdown to Disaster, Frank Curran, Gill & Macmillan, 1986
Reality No 7 (DHAC); *Protestant Telegraph; The Derry Journal; The Sunday Observer; The United Irishman; Saoirse-Irish Freedom* (RSF)
War and an Irish Town, Eamonn McCann, Pluto Press, 1st edition, 1974; 4th edition, 1993
Northern Ireland: The Orange State, Michael Farrell, Pluto Press, 1976
The Sunday Press; The Morning Star
The Road to Bloody Sunday, Dr Raymond McClean, Ward River Press, 1983
The Londonderry Sentinel
The Politics of Irish Freedom, Gerry Adams, Brandon Books, Dingle, Co. Kerry, 1986

Four Sunday, Bloody Sunday
Based mainly on a pamphlet by the same author, published by Starry Plough Publications (IRSP) to mark the sixth anniversary of the massacre. This one-off 22 page illustrated publication unfortunately contained no bibliography, and therefore names of some publishers and dates of publication are difficult to establish after such a lapse of time
A House Divided, James Callaghan (former British PM)
Internment!, John McGuffin, Anvil Books, Co. Kerry, July 1973
The Sunday Times; ALJ research and press releases; *Private Eye; The Scotsman*; Free Communication Group declaration drafted by Roy Bull of the latter named newspaper; *The Guardian*; pamphlets produced by Catholic clerics Fr. D. Faul and Fr. R. Murray, Dungannon, Co. Tyrone
The Special Powers Act, summary leaflet drafted by the NUS (main points included in Appendix 1)
The Socialist Voice (London left-review)
Low Intensity Operations, General Frank Kitson (British army of occupation in Kenya, Malaya, Cyprus, Ireland etc), Faber, 1971
In Holy Terror, Simon Winchester
The Derry Journal; Starry Plough (Derry)

OTHER SOURCES
British Intelligence and Covert Action, Jonathon Block & Patrick Fitzgerald, Brandon, 1983

The Unionjacking of Ireland, Jack O'Brien, Mercier, 1993

SAS in Ireland, Fr. Ray Murray, Mercier, 1990

Begrudger's Guide to Irish Politics, Breandán O hEithir, Poolbeg Press, 1986

Breaking the Deadlock, Robert Heatley (stockist: Irish Freedom Press)

Bloody Sunday in Derry: What really happened?, Eamonn McCann, Maureen Shiels & Bridie Hannigan, Brandon Books, Dingle, Co. Kerry, 1992

That Audacious Traitor (history of the Clann ÓDochartaigh from 1333), Brian Bonner, Salessian Press Trust, Pallaskenry, Co. Limerick, 1985

The Irish War, Irish Freedom Movement, Junius Publications Ltd, 3rd edition, 1987

The Irish Troubles: A generation of violence, 1967-1992, J Bower Bell, St Martins Press, New York, 1993

The Secret Army (history of the IRA), J Bower Bell, Academy Press, 1993

Ireland: The Key to the British Revolution, David Reed, Larkin Publications, 1st edition, 1984

The Story of the Irish Citizen Army, Sean O'Casey, The Journeyman Press, London & West Nyack, first published 1919, reprinted 1980

Patrick Pearse and the Lost Republican Ideal, Dr Brian Murphy (stockist: Irish Freedom Press)

On Another Man's Wound, Earnie O'Malley, Anvil Books, 1979

The Singing Flame, Earnie O'Malley, Anvil Books, 1978

Guerrilla Days in Ireland, Tom Barry, Anvil Books, 1989

Irish Nationalism, Sean Cronin, Pluto Press, 1983

Ireland: The Propaganda War, Liz Curtis, Pluto Press (stockist: Irish Freedom Press)

Unmanageable Revolutionaries, Margaret Ward, Brandon Press

Brian Faulkner, Andrew Boyd, Anvil Books, Co. Kerry, 1972

Ten Men Dead: The Story of the 1981 Irish Hunger Strikes, David Beresford, Grafton Books, London, 1987

On the Blanket: The H-Block Story, Tim Pat Coogan, Ward River Press, Dublin

The Armagh Women, Nell McCafferty, Co-op Books, 50 Merrion Square, Dublin 2, 1981 (taken off the shelves, apparently only in the six occupied counties, following legal action)

My Fight for Irish Freedom, Dan Breen, Anvil Books, Tralee, Co. Kerry, 1964

The First Dail, Maire Comerford, published by her 1916 comrade and

defender of Mount Street Bridge, the late Joe Clarke, 68 Upper
O'Connell St, Dublin, 1969

Beating the Terrorists, Peter Taylor, a Penguin special, Penguin
Books, 1980

Political Murder in Northern Ireland, Martin Dillon & Denis Lehane, a
Penguin special, Penguin Books, 1973

A Citizens' Inquiry: The Opsahl Report on Northern Ireland,
published by The Lilliput Press, Arbour Hill, Dublin and
Initiative '92 (Belfast)

ACKNOWLEDGEMENTS

The author wishes to thank Bernadette McAliskey (née Devlin) for kindly writing the foreword to this work during a period of illness. Also the Irish Freedom Press (41 Arran Quay, Dublin 7) for their extensive book list and information on previous authors and titles. Thanks is also due to Fr. Sean McManus and the Irish National Caucus, Capitol Hill, Washington DC for providing lists of the main Irish-American newspapers and magazines. Fr. Des Wilson and his community team in Belfast for providing similar information on US groups. Individual members of the O'Doherty Clann in New Zealand, Australia and North America who expressed an interest in promoting this work are not forgotten. Assistance by their Clann Herald at their World HQ on Inch Island, Co. Donegal was also most helpful, as was mention of this work in their international newspaper Ar nDuthchas (Our Heritage). The assistance of my schoolteacher friend Vincent Power and my ever-alert mother Mary Ellen in proof-reading the first draft of this and other MS proved invaluable, as such a task is much appreciated by most writers who rarely see their own mistakes. Others not recognised, for various reasons, are remembered also with fondness and gratitude by the author. A big thanks to all the staff of AK Press / AK Distribution in Edinburgh who recognised this writer as a potential first-time author, especially Bob Goupillot who did a fine job of editing and encouraged elaboration of various sections. Also their colleague in Leeds who designed the cover and lay-out, as well as their US representative in San Francisco who took on the mighty task of distribution and promotion across the vast United States. To others, who may be unknown to me, engaged in the various aspects of this worthy field of human endeavour, I extend my sincere thanks also.

Milé buíóchas d'achan duine a chuidigh liom

The author's share of the proceeds from the sale of this book will go towards defraying expenses incurred by the West Bank Research & Development Group which is a voluntary body aimed at tackling high levels of unemployment via individual and collective self-help activities within working class communities in Derry.

SOME RECENT TITLES FROM AK PRESS

BAD
James Carr with an introduction by Dan Hammer
ISBN 1 873176 21 X; 224pp, two colour cover, perfect bound, 6" x 9"; £5.95/$7.95
"When I was 9 years old I burned down my school." So begins the searing autobiography of a former child prodigy of crime in the streets of LA's ghettos. He relates his story with cold passion, illuminating daily life on the streets and in prison. First published and banned in 1975, this is its first reprinting.

TELEVISIONARIES
THE RED ARMY FACTION STORY 1963-1993
Tom Vague
ISBN 1 873176 47 3; 112pp, two colour cover, perfect bound, 5½" x 8½"; £4.50/$6.95
"It was all very *vague*. We talked about Vietnam and then we moved on to other things." — Hans-Joachim Klein, RZ.
A fully revised and updated version of Vague's seminal journey through the RAF.

END TIME: NOTES ON THE APOCALYPSE
G A Matiasz
ISBN 1 873176 96 1; 320pp, four colour cover, perfect bound, 5½" x 8½"; £5.95/$7.00
A first novel by G A Matiasz, an original voice of slashing thought-provoking style.
"A compulsively readable thriller combined with a very smart meditation on the near-future of anarchism. *End Time* proves once again that Sci-Fi is our only literature of ideas." — Hakim Bey.

NO PITY
Stewart Home
ISBN 1 873176 46 5; 144pp, mono cover, perfect bound, 5½" x 8½"; £5.95/$12.95
With this collection of 9 short stories, Mr Home gives fiction back the bad name it deserves.

STEALWORKS
THE GRAPHIC DETAILS OF JOHN YATES
John Yates
ISBN 1 873176 51 1; 136pp, two colour cover, perfect bound, 8½" x 11"; £7.95/$11.95
A collection to date of work created by a visual mechanic and graphic surgeon. His work is a mixture of bold visuals and minimalist to-the-point social commentary, involving the manipulation and re-interpretation of culture's media imagery.

AK Press publishes and distributes – to trade and retail – a wide variety of radical literature. For our latest catalogue, featuring these and several thousand other titles, please send a large self-addressed, stamped envelope to:

AK Press
22 Lutton Place
Edinburgh, Scotland
EH8 9PE, Great Britain

AK Press
PO Box 40682
San Francisco, CA
94140-0682